"In my 25-year career as a businessman, the [...] *have provided such indelible lessons, which challenged my boundaries, built unthinkable confidence, and elevated my personal brand. Thank you Tamara, for being one of those rare, yet special people."*

—Thomas G. Kolaras, Founder, SteelCut Marketing

"Tamara Jacobs is a brilliant strategist in the craft of drawing out a person's singular, authentic voice. Time and again, I have marveled at her superhuman sensitivity to the nuances of self-representation."

—Loreen Arbus, Producer/Writer, Author, Philanthropist

"Tamara is focused, driven, and committed to the improvement and success of others. Having worked with her on key projects over 10 years has advanced the skill set of many. Each encounter is tailored and success is measured by the application of learning to advance a desired outcome. Tamara is world class and has helped develop a plan and provided the coaching and learning for those to execute that goal."

—John R. Burgfechtel, Senior Vice President of Sales, totes»ISOTONER

"Tamara is an amazing talent. I have seen her work communication miracles...I view her as a 'communication surgeon.' Tamara assisted me in many National Sales Meetings, which are both expensive and very important in creating commitment to the future of a product and the company. The success or failure young people experienced from their role in presenting to a large audience played a huge role in developing self-confidence. Tamara's impact on these early career experiences was absolutely amazing. I have seen her transform nervous and no confidence into confident, impactful young managers. To say it's miraculous may be an overstatement, but its close. Finally, I attribute Tamara's role in my successful career as a major factor. Even though I am now retired, I have recommended her recently to help a CEO whose skills need surgery!!!!!"

—Larry Pickering, Former Chairman of Global Healthcare Partners, Credit Suisse, Private Equity, LLC; Former Chairman of Worldwide Consumer Pharmaceuticals, Johnson & Johnson

"As I transitioned to a highly challenging new career, Tamara personally tutored me on the art and science of making great first impressions, of communicating 'smart and capable' by simply walking in the door. But Tamara Jacobs is far more than a coach. She is a brilliant, talented woman and leader. Her guidance and her fine example continue to assist me in realizing my potential every day."
> —Alice P. DiMarzio MS FRICS, Senior Managing Director,
> NGKF Capital Markets

"Every time I leave one of Tamara's seminars I always walk away feeling empowered and able to take on the world! She delivers incredible insights and knowledge in such a clear and compelling way that not only are these valuable lessons retained, they are immediately applicable. Working with Tamara has definitely elevated my ability to impact my audience, and has taken my professionalism to the next level."
> —Ildiko E. Juhasz, LVMH Fragrance Brands, National
> Education Director

"'Hope is not a strategy'; 'Success is a planned event.' These are two of the Tamara-isms that I live by. I have been working with Tamara Jacobs for 18 years and it is one of the best relationships I have both personally and pro-fessionally. She is a master at her trade and anyone that is fortunate to work with her should be ecstatic. Working with Tamara is like hitting the lottery because you really feel like a winner!"
> —Gina M. Liebhauser, Managing Partner,
> Piemonte & Liebhauser, LLC

"Tamara is one of the most preeminent experts to help top executives develop their executive presence in the office and on the stage. I've seen her work successfully with executive teams to help them develop high level corporate messages and visions for their organizations. She has an exceptional knowledge of business and she understands what it takes to be successful in the C-Suite."
> —Pamela Harris-Young, Retired Senior Pharmaceutical
> Executive, Pamela Harris-Young Visight Associates LLC

"In knowing Tamara Jacobs for 20-plus years, she has always demonstrated the ability to identify problems, examine them thoroughly, and develop the best course of action to achieve real and meaningful outcomes. A successful strategist must have keen insight and sound judgment, both of which cannot be taught, but must be innate—Tamara possess both. As a business owner, counselor, and professor of law, Tamara's quick-witted "tell it like it is" delivery and unmatched communication strategies have proven to be extremely valuable in my overall development and growth."
—Patricia Lawrence, Esq., PLK Law Group

"Tamara Jacobs…was by far and away our most expert facilitator. Her interactive style and overall advice for our graduate students— who are emerging leaders in the fields of public policy and urban planning—were exceptional. Tamara gave them superb short and long-term 'take-away' items upon which to act. I am witness to the transformation that has evolved with our students, having integrated Tamara's strategies into their 'toolkit' including embracing the I.C.E.D. mantra. Tamara's advice and strategies are second to none!"
—Hillary M. Bardwell, Assistant Director of Career
Services and Alumni Relations,
Edward J. Bloustein School of Planning and
Public Policy, Rutgers,
The State University of New Jersey

"Working with Tamara Jacobs for the last five years has been and continues to be an inspiration. With our mutual clients, I see her coach them to become…more effective leaders. Her creative contribution and coaching style is collaborative and encouraging not only with our mutual clients and also with my team. Tamara is the real deal!"
—Dorothy Devlin, Co-Founder,
DEVLINHAIR Productions, Inc.

"After reading Be the Brand *I am excited to delve into her latest work. Tamara shares knowledge and nuance on ways to continually evolve as a professional, and to live the "brand" of your organization, and become a leader within your team. Instead of a disposable commodity."*
—Ayette Jordan, Director of Development—Metro NY,
Lubin House, Syracuse University

TAMARA JACOBS

YOUR
ULTIMATE
SUCCESS
PLAN

Stop Holding Yourself Back
and Get Recognized,
Rewarded, and Promoted

CAREER
PRESS

YOUR ULTIMATE SUCCESS PLAN
TYPESET BY EILEEN MUNSON
Cover design by Rob Johnson/Toprotype
Printed in the U.S.A.
The following phrases are trademarked and protected under copyright law:
Don't Honk the Wrong Horn
ComYOUnicate
Role of Receivership
Success Is a Planned Event
I.C.E.D.

To order this title, please call toll-free 1-800-CAREER-1 (NJ and Canada: 201-848-0310) to order using VISA or MasterCard, or for further information on books from Career Press.

The Career Press, Inc.
220 West Parkway, Unit 12
Pompton Plains, NJ 07444
www.careerpress.com

Library of Congress Cataloging-in-Publication Data
Your ultimate success plan : stop holding yourself back and get recognized, rewarded, and promoted / by Tamara Jacobs.
          pages cm
Includes bibliographical references and index.
ISBN 978-1-60163-366-8 (alk. paper) -- ISBN 978-1-60163-386-6 (ebook : alk. paper) 1. Career development. 2. Promotions. 3. Success in business. I. Title.
  HF5381.J4185 2015
  650.1--dc23
                                                                2015010673

Dedication

You can have a great plan, but without great people *Your Ultimate Success Plan* would never have made it from plan to paper. This book is the result of an incredible team of dedicated people who aided, supported, and inspired me to realize my potential and ensure readers will do the same.

Many thanks to family (my mother, sister, daughter, and especially my husband, David—my constant source of strength and most honest critic), friends, clients, and colleagues, and to *you*, my reason for writing this book!

Inspiration

My mother and father; the most original and fearless people I have ever known. She wrote the words, he played the tunes, I sang the songs.

Contents

Part II: Reinvention Tension (Rewarded)
81

Part III: Edge the Ledge (Promoted)
129

FAQs: For Anyone in Doubt

Money is better than poverty, if only for financial reasons.
—Woody Allen[1]

Before beginning this journey, which could lead you toward a path of success beyond your wildest dreams, you might have some questions. I understand; really, I do. Here are a few that might have crossed your mind.

Do I need to go back to school?

No. Much of what you need to know is already inside you. We're not talking about achieving the perfect SAT score, or learning how to calculate the circumference of the moon using river stones and twigs. We're talking about reframing, focusing, and developing your existing skills so that you shine and thrive in a business environment. Though it often feels like it, this is not rocket science. Rather, it's a series of simple steps, watch-outs and behavior modifications that, if implemented by you, will take you closer to realizing some of your much coveted, if not easily attainable goals.

Do I need goals in order for this to work?

Sure, everyone needs goals, but yours can be unique to you. You don't need a burning desire to occupy the "C" suite, or aspire to run your own division, or possess an uncontrollable fixation to lead the team poised to discover the next big cure for athlete's foot. You just need to be clear: whatever you covet—that will make you happy in the act of getting it; and whatever you abhor—that which is standing in the way of what you desire; we will seek to modify your behaviors and increase your awareness and skills so your ability to perceive and adjust on the business playing field improves, measurably!

Is there an end game I should know about?

Of course, there always is! We are going to introduce some concepts and practices that can hopefully (there are no guarantees, after all) eliminate the gap between expectation and results so your view of where your career trajectory is taking you, and where you actually wind up will be one and the same! If addressed and executed as I suggest, you will begin to see results by unlocking some previously locked doors. This stuff works. It's based on insights and methods that I've been sharing in my workshops and in one-on-one coaching with senior executives for years. Others have used my ideas, tactics, and insights put forth here with significant, measurable effect. Trust me, you can do this.

Do I have to be a Millennial to be recognized, rewarded, and promoted?

Nope. No way. This program is for anyone. Whether you're just starting out, have recently begun your middle management phase, are closer to being the boss than you might think, or have hit the glass ceiling and have begun thinking about life after now, the skill sets in this book will serve at any level as important additions to your tool box. A further note about being a Millennial: We live in an age when it's never been a better time to be young. Youth culture is revered now more than ever, and many media companies, dot coms, even old guard, previously un-changed institutions, like automotive, banking, insurance, and big pharma, are seeking a younger, diverse, plugged in, tech-savvy workforce. *But*, experience, talent and track record still translate into bankable skills! That means everyone, no matter what your age, background, belief systems, or history, has an opportunity to get recognized, rewarded, and promoted! You just have to know who you are and what's expected of you every step of the way.

I'm really busy. How much time is this going to take?

I'm a very busy person and so are you. At least we're as busy as we think we are! I understand I have to get and hold your attention before life gets in the way. But, we make time for what's important. In that light, this book is designed to engage you with information at the outset, which can help you begin to transform your habits, your perception, and your focus, which will ultimately positively impact your professional experience. The material is designed to ensure that at any step along the way, if you stop, there will be tips, insights, and takeaways that you can put into practice immediately. But you won't want to stop. If you're like others who have been coached by me, have come to my seminars, and have read my first book, you'll refer to this work often and turn to it over time, again and again. Like a good mentor, I'll be here for you when you need me the most. In fact, you'll even be able to seek additional content online. This material is too important and my desire to assist you in unlocking your full potential is too great for me to not use every tool in my toolbox to help you achieve.

What if I don't want to be rewarded, recognized, and promoted?

That's a great question. Fear of success is almost as pervasive as a fear of failure. Our limiting behaviors are sometimes more challenging to eliminate because we've taken a lifetime to cultivate them. Don't worry! Whether you're an overachiever hell-bent on taking over the corner office, or a more laid-back person who feels intimidated by success, we're going to help you be the best you without putting pressure on you to become someone you're not.

"Do I dare? With a bald spot in the middle of my hair."

—T.S. Eliot[2]

Somewhere between self-help and self-promotion lies self-awareness and advancement. *Your Ultimate Success Plan* is a book that provides easy-to-apply business strategies in an approachable, actionable, authentic way, encouraging you to find your voice and realize your potential.

Remember: Life is a continual sales call. Buy from me, date me, elect me, promote me.

In this book you will learn to:

➲ Build your brand (get recognized).

➲ *ComYOUnicate®* your worth while enhancing your self-worth (get rewarded).

➲ Elevate the status of you (get promoted).

Introduction

Make Every Day Independence Day!

"We Have Met the Enemy and He Is Us!"[1] This clever paraphrase of Commodore Perry's famous quote (made even more famous in the Pogo comic strip) is an apt description of how so many of us self-sabotage on a daily basis, especially at work. Bright, intelligent, competent people have their success thwarted at every turn because of the way they approach common to complex situations with conditioned, defensive, and even self-destructive behaviors.

No matter where you're from, every country celebrates some kind of day of independence—usually from the monarchy that originally colonized it. In the United States, we declared our independence from Great Britain in 1776 and have been shooting off fireworks on July 4th ever since. What's so ironic about our "land of the free" is that so many of us are still slaves to our own inability to shed behaviors that stand in the way of our professional success. Either because of our insecurities, upbringing, culture, or even schooling, we hang onto the very things that prevent us from elevating our performance to achieve our potential. *Your Ultimate Success Plan* will help you recognize the familiar pitfalls that we are all victim to, expose them for what they are, how they hold you back, and declare the benefits you will reap once you declare your independence!

How often have you heard a colleague (or yourself) say, "Money is getting so tight—I hope I get a decent raise this year, "or "My old boss was so great, I hope the new guy will appreciate me," or "I really need to do well on this exam to get the company to pay for this course. I hope I get an 'A'." Sound familiar? Well, the truth is, hope is not a strategy, and by merely hoping, the hapless individuals above will surely be raise-less, date-less, and A-less! The goal of this book is to guide the reader through everyday situations and turn hope into concrete desired outcomes.

One of my trademarked mantras is "There is no satisfaction or security in the status quo." Change is difficult for most people. Left to our own devices, most of us would never change—it's too threatening, too complicated, and too difficult. This is especially true in so many business environments. Merely utter the "C" word and everybody runs for cover. However, rarely, over the course of one's professional life, do things stay the same— yet we still employ the safe, tired methodologies to deal with the issues that come our way (which is usually either do nothing and "hope" things turn out well, or react defensively—neither of which is good)!

It's interesting to note that when clothes no longer fit us (we gained or lost weight, or grew a couple of inches) we go out and buy new ones. We don't keep wearing things that are much too small or much too big, and "hope" they'll look okay. The same should apply to our strategies for living, which no longer fit due to a variety of changes for a variety of reasons. Yet time and time again, I see individuals default to "victim" status because it's easier to hope to be rescued when dealing with adversity than try to make behavior changes. I hear people constantly minimizing their needs and apologizing because they think that will make people like them more. I witness endless passive-aggressive behavior to motivate, because so many are afraid to be transparent and demand what is needed for a specific purpose. I have watched clients confuse assertive behavior with out-and-out aggression (in the long run, bullying doesn't work). A pet peeve of mine is listening to people vent and complain with no attempt to provide any sort of solution (as long as I complain, I've registered my distain and no longer have any responsibility for the issue). So many just can't get past themselves; they make every issue solely about them, ignoring the fact that inclusion drives alignment and enlists people to act.

The "characters" you will meet as well as the stories and anecdotes you will read in each chapter of this book will be quite familiar, I'm sure: women and men plagued with the "Cinderella" Complex—waiting to be rescued; the insecure who trade in their core identity to get others to "like" them more; the perennial complainers who merely want to vent, not solve; the passive-aggressive "sharers" who are afraid to put a stake in the ground; the overly modest who are satisfied with the scraps they are thrown; and many more. They all have one thing in common: the inability to function at the highest level—and it's their own doing!! As Mark Twain observed, "A man cannot be comfortable without his own approval."[2]

Though I have been accused of being somewhat obsessive in my approach to business, the fact is, I just don't leave anything to chance. I'm a firm believer in focusing on the things I can control, and I am proud to say that it's worked out rather well.

I have conducted thousands of workshops and keynotes in my career. And to this day, I still send out a detailed requirements list to all clients, describing the audience, outlining the venue, AV needs, and so on. I always arrive on site with plenty of time to adjust the room setup, walk the space, make sure the technology is working, and have a backup plan if it isn't. I rehearse my keynotes and overviews again and again to ensure they're as flawless as they can be. You'd think that after all these years; I could just breeze in and do the job with my eyes closed. Success simply doesn't work that way. I still spend hours re-arranging conference rooms, testing equipment, and practicing my programs. My equity is my brand, and I work very hard to keep it highly regarded, and therefore, respected.

What I find quite amazing is that so many people experience their careers, day by day, figuratively, with their eyes closed, creating obstacles in their business life. Too much is either left to chance, with power abdicated, or put in the hands of others. *Your Ultimate Success Plan* is devoted to exposing these pitfalls with constructive strategies for elevating personal empowerment. You're not splitting the atom, believe me, but it does require a plan of action. As former Chairman of the Joint Chiefs and Secretary of State Colin Powell said, "Always focus on the front windshield and not the rearview mirror."[3]

In my previous book, *Be the Brand*, I provided a step-by-step series of methodologies on how to develop your personal brand that elevated the readers' ability to inform, persuade and drive action. I have coached professionals at all levels and every walk of life who have struggled with their careers, stuck in jobs they really didn't enjoy. They hung on to the well-intentioned, but debilitating advice of family and friends, scared to make the "wrong" choices and disappoint others. *Your Ultimate Success Plan* liberates the reader (you) to be able to make beneficial, productive choices and shop your brand to achieve desired outcomes on your terms.

The individual in my life who turned me on to the concept of applying simple strategies to make beneficial productive choices (and outcomes) was my mother. Annette Jacobs was an aspiring gourmet cook and maintained a beautiful home for our family in suburban Michigan. However, we were incredibly unappreciative of her efforts—to the point of occasionally ridiculing the elaborate meals she prepared for us. Initially, she was put out, but then realized that playing the victim was not working for her—and what would work was *paid* work and employers who would show their appreciation with a salary! So, to the horror of her family (we had become quite accustomed to rumaki appetizers and chicken cordon bleu) and to the embarrassment of my father, who believed a woman's place was in the home, she left home to "shop" herself to the newly created community college.

My mom saw a need and told them she could fill it. You see, in addition to being an amazing cook, she had several advanced degrees that she decided to showcase as she went about the business of re-branding herself. Mrs. Jacobs was about to become Professor Jacobs. She called the dean and sold herself over the phone. My mom didn't know it, but she was about to apply what's called the "challenger selling skills model" (recognize a problem, provide a solution). During their subsequent lunch she informed him the school was lacking a speech department, and that she could create it, design the curriculum, and wouldn't mind conducting class in a WWII Quonset Hut. With a total campus enrollment of eight hundred, Annette became one of only seven full-time faculty (and the only female). Twenty-six years later, my mother retired as one of the most popular and respected pillars of the teaching staff, loved by students and colleagues, the author of articles and winner of state and national excellence awards. With no "self-barriers" to tell her not to, my mom simply saw an opportunity and went for it. She shattered glass ceilings and wasn't even aware of it. Her mantra has always been "Don't let other people define you!"

Fast forward two decades and two generations to my daughter, Avery. Brilliant and iconoclastic, her middle school years provided her with a painful experience and a defining moment—a life lesson she shared in her college admissions essay and the inspiration for this book.

Avery's College Admissions Essay

"If one advances confidently in the direction of his dreams and endeavors to live the life which he has imagined, he will meet with a success unexpected in common hours.

—Henry David Thoreau (Walden)[4]

I am choosing to start my essay with a quote, because I feel that all great ideas and decisions come as the product of one of three things: society's influence, the perception of others and self-discovery. Throughout my life I feel lucky to have been impacted by a combination of all three.

But, let's get back to the quote. Thoreau eloquently sums up what most of us are taught from a young age—which is to pursue our dreams. What I love about quotes is how they can be interpreted—for example, if someone were to ask my mother about this quote, the first thing she would notice is how Thoreau writes his quote in masculine terms, using "his" and "he." My mother has always been an advocate of women in leadership, and the position of women in the workforce.

This leads well into my primary point about society's influence. As a child the first people we learn from are our parents. Being the only child of smart and successful parents, I learned from a young age the importance of being an overachiever. My mother always taught me to never let anyone discourage or discriminate against me because of my gender, age, or opinions. Whereas my father taught me that one has to work hard for everything he/she gets.

Though I was sheltered in grammar school by my parents and a nurturing learning environment, I was hit with a different interpretation of social influence when I reached middle school. My parents have always encouraged me to do what I want and try everything—so it was a culture shock to me when I was suddenly being ridiculed for asking too many questions, sitting in the front of the class, or missing out on free time to go and get extra help from my teachers.

It was at this moment that I faced one of my biggest dilemmas—should I cave and conform to society's (in this case, my friends') beliefs regarding how I should act and dress, or should I continue to do what I believed and stay true to myself.

It was then and there that I realized that I was an individual—and instead of conforming to trends, I would SET them."

...and so can you!

Part I

The Reason *to* Believe (Recognized)

Chapter 1

Success Is a Planned Event!

People believe the only alternative to randomness is intelligent design.

—Richard Dawkins[1]

Mission Statement
In order to devise the right plan, intelligence needs to be gathered, conditions on the ground need to be assessed, decisions need to be made.

Excuse my impudence for saying so, but if you want more out of your work life, then there is no more important place you can be than right here, reading this line in this book, right now. Everything else in your life can wait, even for a little while, and most certainly will be there when you put the book down. What being here now tells me is that you've decided it's time to take a more productive, committed, engaged, and possibly a more proactive role in architecting your success. In doing this you are dramatically improving the odds that being recognized, rewarded, and promoted is within your grasp now, or in the near future.

Whether you know it or not, reading these words reaffirms a commitment you've made to yourself, your family, your colleagues, and even your friends because you've made a determination that the status quo isn't working for you any longer. Or maybe you're not quite at that realization yet, but you're close to deciding there must be a better, more enriching, more satisfying, more lucrative work life than the one you're experiencing. It's okay. You're not alone. But sometimes, pulling the switch and acting on your desire is a challenge.

It's true for many of us that we often don't seek to go from point A to point B unless we're unhappy at point A. Complacency and a lack of quality motivation affect us on so many levels. Our careers often suffer from a lack of informed planning and direction that can make a significant, lasting, and profound impact on our lives. I'm not just talking about your earning power or your title. I'm talking about the kind of fulfillment and joy that come from being in the right company, at the right time, doing something you're good at.

Having a success plan makes sense. The fact that you're reading these words tells me that the idea of designing a plan for success resonates with you. After a long week at work don't we often have a plan for Friday night? Perhaps it's drinks and dinner, or maybe some take-out and binge-watching the latest hit series on Netflix. Either way, there is forethought and execution (i.e., a plan). Sadly, it's true for many of us that it's easier to figure out brunch on Sunday than it is to decide what to say to your boss on Monday.

Success at work doesn't have to be something that happens to others. Successful planning doesn't have to be fraught with doubt, worry, and self-judgment. For all the people out there who seek a more profound life full of wealth and recognition you need to realize there's always someone else who's got more money and more accolades. Your success isn't in the getting of things; it's about living the life of your dreams, no matter what they are. So, in the spirit of really going for it, there are seven concepts ("isms") that I'd like to address. Seven seems to resonate, like seven days of the week, the seven seas, and seven colors of the rainbow.

1. Success is a choice.

Tamara (my name) combined with the suffix -**ism** (a distinctive practice, system, or philosophy) has made for some pretty useful, if not handy portable sayings, that over time help reinforce the bigger theme and materials I've designed to help you be more successful.

"ism" isn't a four letter word!

These "isms" are about how you step up to truly maximize your potential to get ahead. Simple is memorable. Mantras turn into missions. They are the "ear worms" that will earmark your trajectory from cubicle to corner office. Before I go on to my second Tamara-ism, I think you should know a little something about me: I love these short, quippy, easy-to-remember sayings that sum it all up, quickly and succinctly. I've even trademarked some of them. At my core, I'm a teacher, and if there's one thing that has motivated me to create a set of takeaways that are easy to remember, it's that my students—many of them executives—lose their focus and attention more easily than children running wild at Disneyland. We're all guilty of starring in our own production of short-attention-span theater. There's no judgment in being busy, having a full workload, and being distracted, so I had to adapt my game *and* my approach if what I was teaching was going to resonate and stick with my clients. In the spirit of sustainability, let me next share my second and perhaps most profound Tamara-ism with you. In fact, it's so important that it is the title of this chapter!

2. Success isn't a random act. *Success Is a Planned Event!*

It means that planning, anticipating, analyzing, and acting on opportunities can take you to new heights. Successful people do many of the same things consistently. Part of planning for your success includes taking stock of what others do who are successful. For example, most successful executives have energy and enthusiasm in overdrive. They often get up early and have energy to burn at the end of the day. Their enthusiasm is infectious. They jump higher and move faster than others. They also have a quality—call it a character trait—that makes other people want to be like them, or be near them. Their persona is captivating and inspiring. You too can be the kind of person who others look up to, admire, and respect. All of these qualities, by the way, might lead you into the realm of being recognized, rewarded, and promoted, which leads to another important factor that you need to know now.

3. You can only be the best you.

Trying on someone else's shtick isn't going to cut it, because these days being authentic and being transparent are buzzwords that matter the most. As Oscar Wilde said, "Be yourself because everyone else is taken."[2] In today's distracted and device-addicted society in which everyone is looking down, the need to step up and stand out has never been harder or more important. So I would add, "Be yourself and exploit your uniqueness."

4. The past is history; the future is mystery.

I told you at the beginning of this book that we were not going to try and remake you into the image of someone you're not. It's crucial that, as we begin our journey together to help you devise *Your Ultimate Success Plan*, you understand the following: You already have everything you need inside of you to be a success. Think about it for a moment. This isn't a motivational pitch I'm trying to sell you in order to boost your ego. Nor is it an empty sentiment designed to engage you at a rudimentary level. Helping *you* devise a success plan so that *you* can achieve recognition and get rewarded and promoted is the goal of this book. The path you're going to follow, at least in part, is marked by *your* successes and failures up until this point. As self-help guru Wayne Dyer said, "The past is simply the trail you leave behind you."[3] True, the past might also be an indicator of future performance, but only if we allow it to be so. In the best case, the past should inform the future no matter if past behaviors are to be embraced and amplified or if self-limiting behaviors are to be identified and jettisoned.

The notion that your life experience has been the perfect testing ground for what might come next in your professional pursuits is based on my personal experience observing others. Let's say it's the by-product of my observations as an employee, executive, coach, mentor, and friend. What I've learned is: Your instincts, training, background, family of origin, survival skills, and unique perspective—all the qualities that shape you—are exactly the attributes that are going to allow you to shine and spotlight your success at work. The opposite is true for bad behaviors, or actions on your part that are limiting to you and others.

5. Implement vs. Complement.

The more you implement action that does not serve you and others (the more you are unwilling to look at the big picture and understand what's going on around you), the higher the probability you'll be doing things that don't complement your new goal of being recognized, rewarded, and promoted.

It's great to have a goal, and the subtitle of this book has been designed as a three-part plan to give you successive feedback on the work you're doing. These three overarching "lanes" address the physical law that for every action there is an equal and opposite reaction—meaning, if you do well, excel, up your game, learn the rules of the road (depending on the highway you're traveling) put in the time, and add just a bit of luck, good things can happen for you.

6. Hope is not a strategy.

One of the defining aspects of whether or not good things will happen for you—and good things will happen not because you hope they do—is because you've worked hard to make the adjustments that are crucial if you're going to make your success a reality. Part of what will determine the course of natural events in the future is being able to unleash the true talent, ambition, and winning personality that lie within you.

7. What you already know best, I can't teach you.

For heaven's sake, the first American in orbit was a chimp named Ham! You heard me. Our first astronaut was a primate. He didn't actually fly the *Mercury* capsule, but he did sit there quietly. Good Ham. I think his mission profile was to stay alive and not push any buttons to crash the capsule!

The point is, we can teach almost anyone to do almost anything, *except* the most important attributes of being a great employee; work ethic, honesty, trustworthiness, integrity, human nature, communication skills, energy, enthusiasm, and innovative thinking are almost impossible to impart to another without a tremendous amount of effort mixed with frustration for good effect.

The reality check is that some of these innate gifts can't be taught without a ready and willing subject who is able to show up and do the work. By "do the work" I mean it's conceivable that anyone with the right attitude can take on and learn some of the beneficial qualities that some were born with and others adopted over time. The first step is having an awareness of what is important, and what is lacking. The key is to develop and reinforce positive traits, whether they are from birth or acquired, that can serve you 24/7. Think of what I'm saying in even simpler terms: Natural-born (or in some cases acquired) talents and personality traits, when combined with teachable skills and learned fundamentals, make for a winning combination that will eventually reap you a tangible benefit.

Your manager can teach you the payroll system, how designs load into that sleek file-sharing system, and how new accounts are opened for clients, but none of these factoids is nearly as important as the skills and abilities you show up with on day one that are the product of your character and life experiences. What you really know and can use to your advantage, and what will benefit your organization, are what you brought to the table long before you were hired. Your guts and your smarts count. So does your ability to read and disarm a foe. Your aptitude of turning deficit to advantage, your sense of right and wrong, and your talent with others all count big time.

These are skills/isms that elevate being an employee to an art form. In that rarefied air is where greatness and great jobs lie. You have value and skills that transcend the workplace. By aligning your natural abilities with your career path, you improve the probability that someone in a position of authority will recognize your strengths and reward you accordingly. Let's make these seven stick and start looking deeper.

As the great ad man David Ogilvy once wrote, your unique value proposition has everything to do with what you love and are passionate about doing and would do even if you weren't getting paid. But for now, however, I suggest that you do get paid. Further, I want to up your compensation. Translation: I want you to be recognized and rewarded for being the best *you* you can be. This is all about you, and a celebration of your talents and abilities is the best place to be as we bring our planning phase into focus.

Answer this question: What do you love to do? Write it down. Answering e-mail, tweeting your friends, and posting pictures on Instagram only count if you're in marketing! Maybe you're great at math, or you're a terrific writer. Some people have a gift interacting with people. Others prefer animals. Are you great in the kitchen? Some love to take photos on shimmering mountaintops; others are capable of producing financial spreadsheets of such depth and perfection that they should be framed. Not everyone is capable of doing everything, and this is never truer than it is at work.

Some might argue that being successful begins and ends with doing what you love. In our world we're going to broaden the definition just a bit. In order to make a success plan that sees you being recognized, rewarded, and promoted, let's agree on some of the tenets that define success.

In fact, because we're developing *Your Ultimate Success Plan*, now's as good a time as any to really decide what success looks like. I've outlined three main aspects that comprise the prevailing notion. It's not perfect, nor is it meant to be definitive. It's just my way of wrangling a broad subject into manageable morsels.

Wealth

Monetary success is not the only way success can show up in your life, but it's not a bad place to start! It's obvious that most of us are seeking some form of financial independence that allows us to the live the "good life" on a purely personal basis. For some, wealth means having a great place to live and a surplus of food. With wealth you can pay the bills on time and pay down your debt. You can invest in the present and future without worrying about your principal. You can run up credit cards bills or put them away forever and pay off your debt every month.

Many aspects of success through wealth are common for all of us. For some, material success might also mean having that Ferrari or Lamborghini in the garage. For others it might indicate a closet full of the holy triumvirate: Prada, Fendi, Gucci. It might also mean that you're free to travel anywhere in the world, to wine and dine to your heart's content. Material wealth is often an indication that something has gone very right in your life, but as famed manager, producer, and executive David Geffen once said, "Anyone who thinks money will make you happy hasn't had money!"[4]

Position

To do well in a business environment and to be successful at work usually means you've done many things right. You've proven yourself capable, you've demonstrated excellence in numerous ways, and you've impressed the powers that be to the extent that you are entrusted to lead other employees. In this regard, success typically means you've got a title and a nice office. You've also got a number of direct reports (people on your staff working under you) and you're being held accountable for the work product your group delivers.

You might have even been promoted a few times. Though promotion doesn't always lead to material wealth, it does often lead to an increase in visibility, viability, and prominence within an organization. Politics become more pivotal. Are you happy? Do you like your team and do they like you? Does your direct boss respect you and treat you with grace under pressure, or is he or she a bully who is prone to unfortunate behavior? Position is a worthy notch on the success belt, but it doesn't always come with material wealth, though the better you do within a company, the more perks you get to enjoy.

Honors

Awards and accolades of any kind are thrilling to receive. They don't pay the bills, but they do afford you the luxury of leveraging their existence into a better deal, more responsibility, or a new role within your organization. We live in a "follow me" culture, where, as famed screenwriter, playwright, and novelist William Goldman said, "Nobody knows anything."[5] He was talking about Hollywood executives and how most of them (it's a dirty little secret in Tinsel Town) wouldn't know a hit movie from "a ham sandwich." That is, until the terrifying shark, alien girl with a bow and arrow or a boy with an ability to play Quidditch becomes a hit. Then everyone is a genius and everyone knows everything. It's the same with honors. Just the very idea that you've won an award or have been given recognition is, by all accounts, not a trivial development. Here's a wakeup call: In business, winning an industry award presents you with a distinct advantage now more than ever.

With social media taking a more prominent role in business, having something to tweet about is important. It makes your clients and colleagues feel they're doing business with an all-star. And because we've already said perception is reality, it's important to realize what people think about you matters more than anything else. So, working hard for the money also means working hard for that little silver plaque that's given out once a year. Your future boss is there too, watching and taking notice. She's the one who's next going to recognize, reward, and promote you. Most likely she's going to accomplish this by stealing you away from your current place of employment. She might have had her eyes on you for some time. The word on the street about you might be more than solid. Or maybe she might be poaching you because your outfit is killer and you just destroyed her team at the annual ad agency awards. You've got to be in it to win it, and being seen is one great way to begin down the road of being recognized and rewarded.

There are plenty of other benchmarks for success including happiness and good relationships at home and at work. Being a good parent, or loving son, daughter, or sibling, all count toward success, in the grand scheme, but for our definition, *Your Ultimate Success Plan* is going to make you a business success, get you a corner office, and present you with a framed plaque.

You can't always get what you want.

Take into account, at least nominally, that sometimes the best-laid plans don't actually come to pass. It happens every day. Part of developing and understanding your plan is allowing for the following: Life isn't always fair. As famously stated by Dale Carnegie, "Our fatigue is often caused not by work, but by worry, frustration and resentment."[6]

There are many factors that determine your viability within your organization:

You might be working in the wrong group for a dreadful boss who's jealous and hates anyone who's better, nicer, more attractive, or more talented. We will address the horrible boss paradox a bit later, but this shaggy dog story is all too familiar to many of us whose best-laid plans have been laid to waste by a less-than-desirable situation. Usually this happens when an outcome—say, a promotion—doesn't line up with a crucial expectation.

You might find yourself in a company where nobody leaves. It happens all too often. Sometimes companies large and small make it too attractive to exit, and with a trusted workforce they don't ever encourage turnover. So, a promotion and anything more than a cost of living raise is out of the question. Maybe the reward is steady employment, a growing 401(k), and that silver plaque everyone wants.

Another factor that's harder to quantify is age. Aging out is a problem. We do live in a youth culture, and though it's against the law, there are times when younger, less-experienced executives get promoted over more seasoned, more accomplished veterans. It's not pretty, but from time to time, it's a fact of life. Maybe the reason given is "Your style just doesn't mesh with the team." Or, "We're thrilled for you to stay on. We just think Chelsea has more vision for the senior director role." Just because you get passed over doesn't mean you have to go to the "dark side." In fact, the opposite is true. If history has taught us anything, it's that from deficit comes advantage.

Just because you have a plan doesn't mean it will work.

As Dwight David Eisenhower once wrote, "... plans are useless, but planning is indispensable."[7] Before he was a two-term president, Eisenhower was the five-star commanding officer who led the U.S. Army as part of the Allied forces, defeating the Nazis in World War II. Among his other achievements, Ike (his nickname) was the Supreme Allied Commander during D-Day, when the allies invaded France at Normandy Beach. This event was the beginning of the end for Hitler and the Axis powers. I'd say a fair amount of planning went into the war effort, but not all the battles he organized went as planned. As is often the case, when planning *anything* be prepared for those plans to change. In preparing for what is certain, we usually bump into uncertainty at an alarming rate.

Part of being recognized and ultimately rewarded and promoted says as much about how you handle setbacks as it does about how you manage achievement. Character can be defined in many ways, but the consistent winning traits include steadfastness, trustworthiness, integrity, honesty, and honor. Character is reflected in what we do and don't do. Complaining and backstabbing are not the signs of good character and will often haunt a prospective candidate who is looking for more in his or her workplace.

Overcoming adversity, such as devising a new plan when the last one failed, is a wonderful trait, something that's highly valued by management teams in companies across the globe. The new term is "strategic agility" and it's being touted more and more as a leadership trait. Planning for success isn't going to bring you success. But executing the plan, and acute mindfulness about what you should and shouldn't be doing, is the first step.

In his seminal work, *The Seven Habits of Highly Effective People*, Stephen R. Covey (he totally tapped into the power of seven) addressed the idea of what makes a successful person. He found that "...almost all the literature in the first 150 years or so focused on what could be called the character ethic as the foundation of success—things like integrity, humility, fidelity, temperance, courage, justice, patience, industry, simplicity, modesty, and the Golden Rule. The character ethic taught that there are basic principles of effective living, and that people can only experience true success and enduring happiness as they learn and integrate these principles into their basic character."[8]

But beginning in the 1920s, perceptions of success were driven by externals more than internals—what Covey might call the "personality ethic." We began to define success with a new set of parameters: personality, the image that is projected to the public, charisma, how the person connects to the public, and how individuals relate to one another. A positive attitude was also determined to be a factor. As a result, such homilies surfaced as: "Your attitude determines your altitude," "Smiling wins more friends than frowning," and "Whatever the mind of man can conceive and believe, it can achieve."[9]

Success has many facets and the notion of it has evolved. Whether you're beginning your road to riches, or are closer than ever, putting together a winning plan isn't as easy or as hard as you might think. In order to effectively make a plan, context is important. You're not going to play the same game in a botanical garden as you are in a roller derby rink. Knowing where you are at all times is an important and necessary component of devising a plan that will deliver on the promise of your new day.

? Test Yourself!

1.	What is meant by *"Success Is a Planned Event?"*
2.	How do natural-born traits with acquired skills make a winning combination?
3.	What is meant by "Do the work?"
4.	From a business perspective, what are three key barometers of success?
5.	What is "strategic agility"?
6.	Describe the differences between the "Character Ethic" and the "Personality Ethic."
7.	Which is more important: planning or planning for change?
8.	Why is context important when pursuing your success plan?

Chapter 2

Don't Honk the Wrong Horn!
Being True to Your Brand

Today You are You, that is truer than true. There is no one alive who is youer than You.

—Dr. Seuss[1]

Mission Statement
Features "tell," benefits "sell."

In my last book, *Be the Brand*, I discussed strategies for building your personal brand equity—something I called "elevating the status of you." Now we're elevating the conversation beyond the brand and focusing on how we can get people to buy what you have to sell. When I was an executive consultant at Johnson & Johnson, the leadership team constantly focused on what we described as "brand essence"—the stand-apart quality that makes consumers seek out a product by name, pay a premium price, continue to use it, and recommend it to others.

"Your brand had better be delivering something special, or it's not going to get the business."

—Warren Buffett[2]

In order to be a name brand, you can't be a "me too." We don't buy acetaminophen, we buy Tylenol; we don't reach for a tissue, we blow our nose with Kleenex; we don't copy, we Xerox. Whether they are known as a noun or a verb, the point is these brands are iconic. I've been teaching impact communication skills for more than 20 years to thousands of individuals and hundreds of companies. After experiencing my training, people don't say they've been coached. When complimented on their ability to impress and persuade, they simply say they've been "Tamarized." Yes, in a way, I too have become a quasi-icon. It's how I rise above the competition and continue to grow my business (attract a following). It's my brand features with demonstrable benefits to my clients that make me a commodity (although I haven't reached the vaulted status of Kleenex yet; I'm still working on it!).

Case in point: When building my original website several years ago (more about electronic/virtual impact later) the designer said that I needed to billboard my brand on the home page and asked me to describe myself in three words. I felt I knew who I was and confidently said, "Well I'm original, I'm fearless, and I'm strategic." Her response was instant and unexpected. "Good for you" she groused. "That's bragging. Nobody buys features, they buy benefits. Try again." "Okay," I stammered. I was a little taken aback that it really was about my worth to "them." How could I have missed this point in all those years training sales representatives how to seal the deal, using the time-honored axiom "features tell, benefits sell." And yet I hadn't applied it to myself. I wasn't seeing myself as a product/commodity that needed to do anything more than advertise my attributes. I thought the benefits would be self-evident. So I put myself in the *Role of Receivership*® (putting yourself in the shoes of whomever is receiving the information). Then I ran it by her one more time. "If I am original, I can make you memorable; if I am fearless, I can advocate for you; if I am strategic, I can get you promoted." "Bingo!" she beamed. "Now I want to buy your brand."

What an epiphany! Give them what *they* need while being true to who *you* are. Everyone is motivated by vested self-interest, that overused expression in corporate America: WIIFM (what's in it for me?). Does your brand make them think, feel, or believe differently (and in a *good* way)? In short, does it motivate them to act?

Some iconic brands have disappeared from our midst because they weren't true to themselves or their intended audience. Through greed, lack of foresight, or, perhaps the most damaging of all, insecurity, they began to promote their wants over the needs of their customers.

> "My name became a brand, and I'd love to say that was the plan from the start. But the only plan was to keep writing books. And I've stuck to that ever since."
>
> —John Grisham[3]

Tiffany & Co. is an example of a company that almost fell off the cliff, but saved itself just in time. In an attempt to broaden their market, Tiffany's changed their strategy and began offering more lower priced, less prestige items in their store. I assume they felt that bringing more entry-level shoppers through the door would evolve them into bigger spenders as time went on. What they failed to realize, however, was that this model alienated their base, as high-end shoppers did not want to patronize a watered-down brand. As a result, their bottom line hemorrhaged until new leadership was brought in, the less expensive merchandise was jettisoned, and Tiffany's went back to strictly catering to those with deep pockets.[4] Other companies have not been so fortunate.

The early 1980's brought a truly innovative low-cost travel service: the "no frills" airline by the name of PEOPLExpress.[5] By using a basic ticket pricing model (if you can believe this, they actually ticketed you on the plane during the flight) and planes with one class of seating (except for overseas flights), every seat was sold for the same price (as opposed to today, when it would be hard to find two seats on any single flight that cost the same).[6] It seems so quaint now. A cart was rolled down the aisle with a cash box and credit card swiper, and everyone paid for their seat as they were hurtling toward their destination—always a game of "Beat the Clock" on those short hops to Boston or DC. There were no fees for carry-ons, and if you checked a bag, they charged you three dollars. Modest charges for food and beverages were also imposed.[7] To give you an idea how inexpensive the tickets were (even in 1980 dollars), one-way fares from New York City to Boston, Pittsburgh, and Washington, DC were $19 (cheaper than driving or taking the bus)!![8] Trans-continental flights to and from California were $89.[9] The biggest bargain of all were flights to Brussels and London, which came in at $149.[10] By focusing on profitable hub routes, the airline became wildly successful. However, the itch to expand became their downfall. The ownership purchased additional routes when it bought Frontier Airlines. This put PEOPLExpress in a huge debt position. While this was happening, their competition upped their game by lowering their pricing models, which allowed them to get close to PEOPLExpress ticket pricing (without the add-ons). Most damaging, the integration of the two airlines, with very different cultures (and customers), did not go well. There were labor struggles and Frontier passengers did not like the "no frills" philosophy so prized by the devoted PEOPLExpress clientele. The huge debt forced the airline to chase the business travelers whose companies were willing to pay higher prices, and placed an enormous debt burden on the carrier. They changed their philosophy (and completely diluted their brand) by adding first-class cabins to their planes, incorporating a bonus program for frequent flyers, and adapting a traditional model for ticket pricing to maximize revenue. This proved to be their downfall. A botched integration and debt pressures forced the sale of Frontier Airlines to Texas Air, and PEOPLExpress went out of business.[11]

Founded in 1948, E.J. Korvette was a money-making department store brand, and did much to define the genre of low-priced merchandise under one roof (a la Costco and Sam's Club). At its peak, it had 58 stores throughout the Northeast and Midwest, focusing on appliances and other hard goods. Their business model thrived with their ability to undercut competitors by establishing themselves as a "retail cooperative" complete with membership cards allowing them to negotiate substantial discounts from their purveyors, undercutting such established competitors as Macy's and Gimbels.[12] Even lawsuits against Korvette's couldn't halt their success; the litigation actually proved to be a major public relations boost for the discounter![13] Not satisfied with its "win rate," the owners saw fit to branch into fashion, as well as establishing their own line of audio components. They did not have either the expertise in these areas or outlets with the right atmosphere to attract the shoppers they were seeking. [14] The financial burden this placed on the company took its toll. Stores were closed and the entire chain went out of business in 1980.[15]

In the late '70s, several Hollywood movie moguls fled United Artists and established a new company: Orion Pictures. The company had no real assets except for the huge success record of their leadership, which between them had garnered three Oscars for Best Picture during their previous three years at UA, which had never been done before. So great was their reputation, that many of their former subordinates at UA joined the new company.[16]

As a team of executives who were perceived as "in," the company soon became a top studio with 15 films in production in its first year with some of the biggest stars of the day (such as Burt Reynolds, Peter Sellers, and Barbara Streisand), as well as directors (Blake Edwards, Francis Ford Coppola) and producers (Ray Stark).[17] After only a year, Orion had established themselves as a huge motion picture brand.

Despite a string of Oscar-winning successes (*Silence of the Lambs, Dances With Wolves, Amadeus*),[18] Orion's management decided it was not satisfied with its achievements and needed to broaden its footprint (and brand) by getting into the distribution business through the acquisition of Filmways (a major movie and television distribution company) as well creating a whole new television and cable movie production unit.[19] Here again is an example of the hubris of a company over-expanding their reach and taking on too much debt. They were doing very well, but some misguided executives felt it wasn't good enough. The financial strains took their toll on the studio as they entered and exited bankruptcy proceedings.[20] Despite many critically successful films, Orion could not sustain itself. Things got so bad that their dire financial situation was belittled from the stage of the Academy Awards by host, Billy Crystal. Eventually, the top creative people departed the studio, it was sold to MGM,[21] and it was never again a major creative force.

What PEOPLExpress, Korvette's, and Orion have in common is the fact that they were all major players in their respective industries, and initially did extremely well, even becoming part of the American lexicon. The decision to stray from their brand was fraught with peril and foreshadowed their downfall. If the aforementioned resisted the urge to unnecessarily expand their offerings and dilute their brand, they'd quite possibly still be around today. You are almost always better served by maintaining and exploiting your focus (like Apple). And the same pertains to people.

> "To be in business today, our most important job is to be head marketer for the brand called You."
>
> —Tom Peters[22]

We often try to act in ways that we think we should or in ways we perceive others need to see us, as opposed to who we truly are, creating a huge disconnect. This applies to our personal packaging, choice of automobile, even the hobbies we pursue to enhance/support our image. The pitfalls of straying from our brand are serious; we must learn how we can maximize our drawing power by being consistent, even as we evolve. The only person I've seen make a successful career out of continually re-branding herself is Madonna—and that has become her brand: constant reinvention!

I have always found that personal experience is a great teacher. When I was consulting a major corporate client that had recently purchased a product they wanted to bring from prescription to over-the-counter, a massive marketing/advertising campaign needed to be developed. I had pretty strong opinions regarding how the campaign should be strategized, which put me at odds with the approach the marketing and advertising agencies were planning to take. To work out the campaign and test their consumer appeal the agencies decided to hold a "war games" session, which would gather all the key stakeholders in a room. At the time, I had never heard of the term "war games," so I asked the advertising lead what the dress code was. She replied, "Oh, you know us creative types—funky casual." Now, everyone who knows me understands that I take my personal packaging very seriously. I have to "walk the talk," so to speak, and I like to think my attention to detail is impeccable. My style is also more formal, which is in direct contrast to today's "business casual" environment. For me, casual means dress pants with a coordinated blazer and an Hermes scarf. That's my brand packaging; it's who I am and how I present myself. At any rate, I decided that I wasn't going to let the ad and marketing people outshine me. I could be as "funky" as the best of them (you can see where this is going). So I went to Soho, a chic section of New York City, and purchased harem pants, drawstring boots, a bomber jacket—the works. (I looked like I was ready to pull off a jewelry heist.) It was clearly not me—but my mission was to be just as "hip" as the others at the meeting. Well, I walked into the "war games" conference room, and wouldn't you know it? Everyone, women and men, was dressed in business suits! I was strategically sandbagged by the advertising lead and looked like a complete idiot. I was self-conscious and, in the process, was silenced. I knew that people "hear what they see" and I had lost my identity, confidence, and credibility. I became a mute rather than stand out and speak up, and I disappeared, uncomfortable and reluctant to voice my opinion and opposition. The agency head had taken me out—or rather, I felt she had. As a result, the group went ahead with a flawed campaign, which ended up costing the client millions of dollars. If I had been authentic, packaged myself accordingly, and not made it all about me and my attempt to look "funky," I wouldn't have ended up in what turned out to be a costume, feeling like a fraud.

Several years ago, I made a momentous decision. I was having a good year, and I wanted to show the world that I had arrived every time I arrived. So what did I do? I went out and bought the biggest and flashiest Jaguar I could find. Never mind that I purchased a used one, because I couldn't justify the cost of a new one. I went crazy anytime someone looked at the car cross-eyed, wouldn't drive it in wet weather (it didn't handle very well), and was petrified of someone hitting it because the cost of repairs would decimate my daughter's college fund. Prior to the Jag, I drove an aging Lincoln Town Car, an old gas guzzler that stuck out of my driveway, it was so long. Though it was a mighty comfortable ride, I got a tremendous amount of ribbing for driving it and, after a while, I decided that it was inconsistent with my image and brand. Tooling around Princeton, N.J., in my Jaguar propelled me into a whole new world of affluent cool—or so I thought. I was so protective of the car, I couldn't enjoy it. And way deep down, I thought maybe I didn't deserve it.

One day, I pulled into the parking lot of a major client and looked for a space that was clearly visible from the CEO's aerie on the top floor of the building. As I walked past his office, he pulled me in and very excitedly told me that I had the best car in the whole lot and how cool I looked driving it, whereupon I took the opportunity to vent all my insecurities with the car. The big boss, whom I will call Bob, turned to me and said, "Stop, stop. You've ruined the whole thing. My vision of your coolness has vanished. Get out and come back when I have forgotten this conversation so maybe I can salvage some of my feelings of respect for you." Although Bob always found a way to make everything about him, I did leave his office feeling somewhat dejected, but also strangely relieved at the same time. I came to the conclusion that the purchase of the Jaguar was not a good one. It represented an ostentation that I really couldn't afford and really didn't need, and conveyed an image that simply wasn't me. I sold it shortly thereafter and went back to my Town Car until I decided that a Lexus SUV was the way to go—and that's been my ride of choice ever since.

I went against one of the foundational practices I discuss in my keynotes and workshops: *Be true to your brand*. The Jaguar represented something I thought I should be, as opposed to who I really was. Clearly, it wasn't serving its intended purpose.

Since buying the Lexus, I experience much more inner peace when I get in the car. I think it suits me well, and if someone dents it, so be it. It truly represents my personal brand, and is more consistent with who I am. Though I may admire a sleek Jaguar from afar, I realize that I truly arrived when I understood that my brand was not enhanced when it honked the wrong horn.

Being inconsistent is a brand killer. People like to know what to expect; it gives them comfort and solidifies that they can count on you. Once you have identified and crafted your brand, why squander all the equity you've built with an unnecessary crap shoot? As I said in Chapter 1, *Success Is a Planned Event*; brand image and reputation either advance it or derail it. Choose wisely.

"You now have to decide what 'image' you want for your brand. Image means personality. Products, like people, have personalities, and they can make or break them in the market place."

—David Ogilvy[23]

No matter what you do in life, your personal brand (your reputation, what you stand for, and your credibility) is your most important asset. If you're an entertainer, or the graduate of a 12-step program, reinvention may be an appropriate opportunity. Otherwise, let your brand do the talking and honk that horn proudly!

? Test Yourself!

1.	Why did PEOPLExpress, Korvette's, and Orion Pictures fail when each began so successfully?
2.	Why do people buy brands based on benefits as opposed to features?
3.	What are some of the ways we communicate our personal brand?

Test Yourself! (continued)

4.	Explain how "making it all about you" can be self-destructive.
5.	Describe your personal brand in three words. Why is each important?
6.	If you would ask a close colleague to describe your brand in three words, would he/she use similar terms to yours? Why? Why not?
7.	Have you ever "honked the wrong horn" in a social or professional situation? What were the consequences?
8.	How important is your personal packaging to communicating your brand? Why?

Chapter 3

Cinderella Had a Fairy Godmother: You Don't!

The harder I work, the luckier I get.

—Samuel Goldwyn[1]

Mission Statement
Unless you're in a Tennessee Williams play, never depend on the kindness of strangers!

It's no coincidence that *Cinderella* recently enjoyed a healthy run on Broadway, this time via Rodgers and Hammerstein, and movie-goers enjoyed a brand-new blockbuster version released by Walt Disney Pictures on the big screen. This ancient tale of victimization, oppression, and eventual rescue has captivated women and men for centuries and still manages to inspire the daydreams of the most determined and talented. The recurring plot is so ubiquitous in real-life behavior patterns that it has its own classification in the Aarne-Thompson tale type index (510A-The Persecuted Heroine).[2]

You'd think after all these years we'd know better, but this dysfunctional aspiration just won't die. Years ago, I was riding in the car with my daughter (who was 8 years old at the time). During the excursion, she blurted out, "One day, I'm going to marry a rich man who's going to buy me a big house and anything I want." In a moment of panic (where did she get this from?) I turned to her and bellowed, "You will *not* marry a man to buy you things. You will become successful in your own right, make your own money, and buy yourself what you want—not dependent on someone else to do that for you!" She initially looked confused (probably reacting to my emotional outburst), but eventually got the picture. Neither her mother nor father subscribed to the "rescue formula" to have wants and needs met. Personal empowerment became our battle cry moving forward with my progeny.

Colette Dowling's landmark book, *The Cinderella Complex*, was published in 1982, but much of it still holds true today. She writes of her own experience,

> I discovered that I did not really want full responsibility for myself; that the idea of having to work for a living for the rest of my life was loathsome; that I wished to escape the necessity of exposing myself to others' abrasiveness, others' hostilities, others' unfair expectations. I wanted people to be nice to me, to see how basically honorable and well-intentioned I was. But these "good-girl" qualities were in direct opposition to other desires: I also wanted to rise in my profession, to travel, to move. This is a stunning moment in a woman's life, when—after she has begun to move out, to expand, to raise her sights—she discovers that the rules have changed and she will no longer be rewarded for her compliance, as she has been, systematically, since she was a little girl.[3]

At the time this was written, mostly women were considered to fall prey to this "complex." But as women became more ubiquitous in the workplace and the economy spiraled downward, many became the major breadwinners and men got a big taste of feeling victimized.

So, although the impetus may not be exactly the same, we see hugely skilled and qualified individuals who, despite a portfolio of accomplishment, fall into the trap of looking to be rescued, with less than stellar results. They can often be found in the following situations:

1. My Godmother/Godfather, the Mentor.

The term *mentor* goes back to Greek mythology and was a character in Homer's *The Odyssey*. In that seminal work, Mentor was described as a teacher, advisor, and inspiration to the protagonist, Telemachus.[4] Thus began a series of famous and fruitful mentoring relationships in the fields of philosophy, religion, politics, business, science, and the arts. Some well-known couplings include Plato and Aristotle, Max Talmey and Albert Einstein, Mahatma Gandhi and Dr. Martin Luther King, Audrey Hepburn and Elizabeth Taylor, Warren Buffett and Bill Gates, and more recently, the surprising and incredibly successful coupling of Tony Bennett and Lady Gaga. With a successful track record and because of the many contemporary challenges in business, the mentoring concept has endured and become institutionalized. Throughout corporate America, mentoring programs abound, as well-meaning, highly-placed executives are paired with high-potential workers to nurture and cultivate their talent. These institutionalized "development" opportunities can be set up as manager-subordinate relationships as well as peer-to-peer. Many companies devote significant time and resources to these programs with the expectation that they will profoundly impact performance, retention, and overall quality of life in the workplace. It was, therefore, no surprise to me when I initially shocked my client base with the notion that "the day of the mentor is dead!"

How did I come to this conclusion that basically undermined one of the long-standing corporate sacred cows? Well, although it sounds great on paper, these mutually enabling relationships often break down into the mentor becoming a Svengali to build his/her own kingdom while the mentee evolves into Trilby, with dependence on his/her mentor to shield and protect them from the ravages of the workplace. All goes well until the mentor is transferred or, worse, fired. Like the *Titanic*, chances are the mentor grabs the lifeboat and the mentee goes down.

> "I have a lot of guides...people whose opinions I really
> respect and who I will turn to."
>
> —Jake Gyllenhaal[5]

This exact scenario happened to a very good friend of mine, whom we'll call Jason. He was a managing director at a very large investment bank and had secured an excellent relationship with his boss—his "rabbi," as he called him. Things were going swimmingly for Jason until he walked into his office to find that his rabbi had been fired. He became even more shell-shocked when he discovered that his boss's temporary replacement was someone with whom he did not get along. However, subscribing to the Cinderella Complex, Jason felt that the situation was indeed temporary and a new boss would come along, but wouldn't you know it, the temporary boss became permanent, and Jason was soon walked out the door as well.

Clearly, my friend's reliance on a fairy godfather/rabbi did him in. Immediately after his old boss departed, he needed to start marketing himself up and down and sideways to build a base of support, and not "hope" someone would come along and rescue him.

Other issues undermine these initiatives as well. Mentees often overestimate what a mentor can do for them, causing inevitable ambivalence, or often disappointment. Executives who are assigned to be mentors aren't always skilled in the process, driving frustration and dissatisfaction. And, even when the mentors are qualified, the guidance they provide quite often doesn't match the mentee's needs.

This is not to say that guidance from more experienced and tenured individuals is never valuable. On the contrary, establishing relationships with wiser and more experienced associates can be extremely valuable when navigating tricky corporate waters. What I am saying is that a single, dedicated mentor is not your fairy godmother/godfather who will be there to rescue you when necessary.

Alternative Plan: Build a network of advisors as part of an overall *Sphere of Influence*. Do not become dependent on one individual; there is no safety in putting your eggs in the basket of one counselor. Creating a relevant *Sphere of Influence* is a valuable exercise and should be imperative for those who are looking to climb the ranks in any organization. Basically, draw a wheel with no more than six spokes. Put yourself in the center of the wheel and, at the end of each spoke, write the name of an individual who is a key player (and someone you feel comfortable speaking/interacting with) in departments or areas with which you interact. It is also important that these "spokespeople" (no pun intended) have no direct authority over your area or supervisory responsibilities—it's critical that their input remains free of any conflict of interest. The individuals in this sphere will become your "kitchen cabinet," a group that you can consult with from time to time, as needed. If one or two leave, you still have the benefit of the others without being tainted by the departures. As people do leave, however, you should try to replace them to keep your sphere fresh and diverse.

2. The Promoting Habits of Horrible Bosses.

Not too long ago, a sadistic film with an A-list cast (Kevin Spacey, Colin Farrell, Jennifer Aniston, and Jason Bateman, among others) called *Horrible Bosses* was released, with the premise that the only way to get rid of a really bad boss was to murder him or her. The movie was certainly no Academy Award winner, though it did ring a bell with audiences who saw it—that so many people are willing to put up with a tremendous amount of needless stress, humiliation, and fear in order to hopefully get a promotion and escape from corporate purgatory. The movie was so successful that a sequel was released in 2014 with most of the original cast intact.

Yes, your boss treats you like dirt and is crushing your soul, but he or she holds the key to your future and has the power to eventually award the prize of a great promotion—as long as you can hang in there. You spend your days and nights hoping it happens sooner or later, as opportunity after opportunity is dangled before you with the promise of eventual liberation. Do you remember the Old Testament story of Jacob, the slave, and Laban, who eventually handed him the prize? You know how the story turned out, and yours will be no different!

> "If you think your teacher is tough, wait until you get a boss. He doesn't have tenure."
>
> —Bill Gates[6]

It's common knowledge: The more desperate you are to get out from under a bad boss, the less likely the promotion will happen, especially if the boss has anything to say about it. Your time is your most precious commodity. Don't waste it on things you can't control and focus on the things you can control.

Alternative Plan: It comes down to this: You have three choices: 1) work to make the situation better; 2) suffer with the status quo; or 3) get out. Actually, going forward the best route is to develop a realistic exit plan as soon as you get a new job. That way, if a horrible boss situation arises again, you won't be left hoping it's going to get better. You will no longer have to attempt to mollify and please a psychopath, and if things don't improve, you will smell the potential for self-loathing and head to a less-scorched pasture. With an exit strategy in place, the boss's leverage is gone and your sense of self-worth remains largely intact.

3. "It's not my fault!"

Although I like to think I'm the first to take responsibility for my mistakes, I know it isn't my forte (or most other people's for that matter). Most of the time, I play the role of adult and manage issues with a certain sense of self-awareness and self-deprecation ("I know I'm deeply flawed," etc.). However, I must admit that there are times when I revert back to my inner "angry child" and point the finger away from me (where it belongs) and aim it at another.

I recall a particular incident in which my fickle finger was directed squarely at my husband. I had to get up early to be at a doctor's appointment, but we both pressed the snooze button on the clock radio once too often; everyone got up late that day. So, we had to rush through our morning ablutions: breakfast, coffee, making lunches, dealing with hair, brushed teeth, backpacks, finding sandals—the usual. With only 10 minutes to spare, I still had to drop my daughter off at school, my husband at work, and get to the doctor. It was then that I launched an attack on my husband: "You know I hate being late! You know I hate being rushed! Maybe it's time you packed Avery's lunch. Maybe it's time you took more responsibility." Blame, blame, blame, blame. I then dropped the poor guy at his office, who couldn't get out of the car fast enough—but hey, I felt justified.

> "Take your life in your own hands, and what happens? A terrible thing: no one to blame."
>
> —Erica Jong[7]

Well, I did make it to the doctor on time, and it wasn't until after my appointment that I began to feel that maybe, just maybe, I had played the blame card much too hard, and began to feel childish. I called my husband's office (he wisely did not take my call) and left a message saying that I felt very sorry for the whole thing and apologized. But I then asked myself: Why did I have to do that? Why was my default reaction to shift the blame away from me? I had as much responsibility to get up early as he did—if not more. After all, I had the doctor's appointment. The simple truth is that I felt ashamed and refused to "own it."

In business, I see this sort of thing all the time. The shame of taking responsibility (and the perception that if we own the fault, it will somehow result in a stain that will never come off) causes us to point the finger at every turn. But does that protect us or do even more damage?

Jill Brown, professor of management at Lehigh University, puts it this way: "Unfortunately, finger-pointing or scapegoating is fairly common, especially recently, as many workers have been feeling insecure about their jobs. When people are insecure, they tend to shirk responsibility for their mistakes."[8]

"A culture of blame can create a very difficult work environment," says Alina Tugend, who writes the Shortcuts column for *The New York Times* and is the author of *Better By Mistake*. Research shows that whether conscious or subconscious, blaming perpetuates and even exacerbates the problem, Ms. Tugend says. "Conversely, when people see others taking responsibility for their mistakes or failures, they also copy that, creating a better overall work environment."[9]

"The last thing you want is a reputation for throwing co-workers under the bus. It's far more politically savvy and productive to approach the mistake as a team problem. Recommend a post-mortem analysis of what happened, where you look at the chain of events, what occurred and what didn't, and questions get answered in a good-faith process," says Ben Dattner, a management consultant and author of *The Blame Game: How the Hidden Rules of Credit and Blame Determine Our Success or Failure.*[10]

Jodi Glickman, president of Great on the Job, a communications training firm in Chicago, explains that by focusing on one person's mistake, little gets accomplished. "It's not about the one error," she says. "It's about the breakdown in communications or the lack of understanding of responsibilities. You can, however, speak privately to the person. Let the person know you are aware that the mistake is his or her responsibility, and ask how you can help prevent it from happening in the future."[11]

Alternative Plan: Accountability and responsibility are important. Once you've personalized the problem and made someone else "wrong," the whole communication chain will break down as everyone goes to their battle stations. Always make it about the problem and not the person. Acknowledge there was an issue, declare there is responsibility for it with the entire group (when one person does something wrong, it's often a communication issue, and communication is a two-way street), and go directly to solution-finding.

As an example, my father would stand in front of the refrigerator when someone had left it open and bellow (in front of the still-open fridge) "Who left the refrigerator open?!" and conduct an inquest while everything started wilting inside. My suggestion to close the fridge while he conducted his investigation was always met with, "Well, I wouldn't have to close it if someone hadn't left it open!" Eventually, we decided that whoever was closest to the fridge when my father began his tirade would take the heat and close it, spreading the blame evenly around, with no specific family member having to own the stain of "food spoiler."

4. He's/she's not perfect but he/she has money.

This is a difficult nut to crack especially when one considers the complex relationship people have with money. It used to be that more women compromised on their relationships when men were the majority breadwinners. Today, with 54 percent of the workforce made up of women, more and more men are ceding the earner role to women and deciding that it's easier to rely on them and be taken care of. However, unlike men who perhaps enjoyed the powerful role of bringing in the money, powerful women are more resentful of their male spouses who, they perceive, don't do enough. And when more women are increasingly in the role of family breadwinner, they save less for retirement than men (career interruptions for family) and are more financially risk averse, even in the early years of investing. It's so much easier to rely on someone else to make the big bucks, so we can overlook a few fatal flaws. This perspective is fraught with peril. Having your own money may not buy happiness, but it does give you choices, *which is critical*. And no matter how close you may become to your partner, his or her money does not necessarily become your money, so you may not have the choices you need.

> "Anybody who thinks money will make you happy, hasn't got money."
>
> —David Geffen[12]

In order to successfully marry for money, you have to bring something to the table—youth, looks, vigor, brains, and so on. Whereas the brains will remain intact, more often than not, the youth, looks, and vigor will fade over time, which is why men of means often trade in their partners for a younger model and women of means become resentful and call a divorce lawyer. Hard to hear, and even more difficult to articulate, but alas, it's true. So the "rescue" will be short-lived at best. Why put yourself in that position?

Alternative Plan: Take a good look at your potential partner without the money. If you don't like what you see, forget it. Though the initial thoughts of financial freedom may be enticing, that "freedom" becomes very costly in other ways and instead of giving you choices, it could potentially make you feel even smaller and more victimized. Partner for love and live on the money you make. More stuff isn't worth it!

There is a pattern here: getting out of difficult situations via a cycle of dependence—on someone else—a mentor, manipulative boss, a wealthy potential spouse. It all comes down to a matter of control. By depending on a rescue, you give up control (and choice) and abdicate all of your power to someone else (or a recurring fantasy, which never comes true).

My daughter had a great time when she went to see the stage revival of *Cinderella*—she loves the music. She was careful to add that she would also love to see a sequel, and find out how Cinderella fares, living at the behest of a "Mamma's Boy" prince and his parents in a drafty castle.

? Test Yourself!

1.	Why is waiting to be rescued a trap?
2	Describe the conflict between women's desire to be liked versus the desire to be successful.
3.	Why do so many companies sponsor mentoring programs? What are the intended benefits?
4.	What is the potential downfall of having a single mentor?
5.	What is a "Sphere of Influence"?
6.	How does the Old Testament tale of Jacob and Laban apply to today's horrible bosses?
7.	What are the three choices one has when working under a difficult supervisor?
8.	When does it make sense to marry for money?

Chapter 4

Apology Not Accepted

*I attribute my success to this—I never gave or took any
excuse.*

—Florence Nightingale[1]

Mission Statement
As soon as we worry about you, your impact and credibility disappear!

We've all heard it time and time again—it could be at the beginning
of a critical one-on-one conversation or a formal presentation—the most
damaging four words one can speak: "Please bear with me." That mis-
placed disclaimer will color everything that follows. Although we all speak
and listen with vested self-interest, the fact of the matter is that no one is
going to be influenced by anything you say or do if you make it about you.
Sympathy is fleeting, and when you appear weak or helpless, your skills to
persuade and drive action immediately evaporate.

Can you imagine that while test driving a car the salesman says, "Sorry,
the ride is usually smoother than this"? Being natural doesn't mean sharing everything, especially information that could potentially damage your
brand. It's not about being withholding; it's about being strategic. And, not
surprisingly, women tend to over-apologize more than men.

Respected psychotherapist and author Beverly Engel notes that, "A fear of conflict is a big reason why many people, especially women, over-apologize."[2]

However, male or female, Engel concludes that reflexively overusing the word "sorry" encourages workers to target and leverage "what they perceive as your weakness...that you're ineffectual and have low self-esteem, which is dangerous knowledge in the wrong hands. It can give a certain kind of person permission to treat you poorly."[3]

> "To be persuasive we must be believable; to be believable
> we must be credible."
>
> —Edward R. Murrow[4]

Whenever we are communicating, either formally during a presentation or informally one-on-one, in addition to providing information to change behavior (persuade, drive action, alter opinions), we are also displaying our brand. Whether we like it or not, each time we get in front of others, we present the sum total of the experiences our audiences have had with us—both good and bad. So even if you don't happen to beg forgiveness for some minor issue in the moment, we still remember all the times you did, and it does erode your credibility.

A very good friend of mine (who happens to be one of the nicest people I know) has a tendency to incessantly apologize, not only for her imagined transgressions, but for everyone else's as well—*and* (remember my mantra regarding the power of repeating: "Repetition Builds Retention") she digs herself in deeper by saying "I'm sorry. I'm so sorry," several times. Whenever I think of her, it's always very fondly, but not as very persuasive. As a matter of fact, I often dismiss her opinions/observations because of her weakened brand.

Suppress the apology reflex!

We have been subjected to an endless parade of "sinners" whose dramatic *mea culpas* provided fodder for talk shows and soft-news broadcasts, but probably one of the biggest apology fiascos in recent memory was by celebrity chef and former Food Network star Paula Deen. Tarred and feathered for her inappropriate use of a grotesque racial slur years ago, she went on an extensive public relations junket, climaxed on the *Today* show when she excused her behavior by telling anchor Matt Lauer that she has used the slur only once, when a gun was pointed at her head by a bank robber 30 years ago. As tears streamed down her face, she biblically exhorted anyone who was "without sin to cast the first stone."[5]

As a public figure, her inability to shed anachronistic behavior resulted in her having to endure a "Scarlet Letter" for her cultural bigotry. What was also so distressing about the whole affair was how she handled it, and her damage-control experts really failed her. What she should have done was admit that what she said was terribly wrong and inappropriate, even under the circumstances; she hadn't used such language since and (putting herself in the "*role of receivership*") will continue to do whatever it takes to regain the respect of her many followers and fans. Going underground, as she did for several weeks, and then performing an extensive public self-flogging eroded her credibility even more, and opened the door for many of her corporate partners (including the Food Network) to make a hasty retreat and cut off their associations. It was a costly error and strategy in more ways than one!

Paula Deen is far from the only woman who fell badly on the apology sword. As we discussed previously, women apologize more than men do. A recent study out of the University of Ontario noted, "it's not that men are reluctant to admit wrongdoing; it's just that they have a higher threshold for what they think warrants reparation. When the researchers looked at the number of apologies relative to the number of offenses the participants perceived they had committed, they saw no differences between the genders."[6]

This is where it gets interesting. Because most people communicate "facing inward" (in other words, they focus on what *they* want to say, how *they* feel, what bothers *them*, as opposed to their audience, one-to-one, or one-to-many), what functions as a transgression needing an apology becomes a self-fulfilling problem. And this study shows that women feel the need to apologize more than men, especially when an audience doesn't feel an apology is necessary or warranted. "Men aren't actively resisting apologizing because they think it will make them appear weak or because they don't want to take responsibility for their actions," says lead study researcher Karina Schumann. "It's just that they think they've done fewer things wrong. Women might have a lower threshold for what requires an apology."[7]

I performed my own focus group and found that most of the women I spoke to apologized to friends, family, and coworkers to avoid confrontation or make the individuals or groups they were speaking to like them better (or dislike them less). Even though they thought they were fixing a situation, they were actually setting themselves up to always be the one at fault. Evidently, it's much easier to take blame than justify behavior.

Many women apologize to please others or avoid conflicts. I would like to think that this is only because women are more connection-focused and care deeply about harmonious relationships. But part of me also thinks that our penchant for apologizing has something to do with our status in relation to men. There is nothing wrong with saying "I'm sorry" when it is rightfully warranted, or to express sympathy, care, and concern for another person. But we should take care to examine our apology, or not apologize, when it undercuts our credibility and confidence.

> "It is a good rule in life never to apologize. The right sort
> of people do not want apologies, and the wrong sort take
> a mean advantage of them."
>
> —P.G. Wodehouse[8]

Then there's the non-apology apology (interestingly used equally by men and women). This is quintessential passive-aggressive behavior that attempts to turn the tables and re-assess blame. We have all been on the receiving end of one of these: "I'm sorry you were insulted." "I'm sorry the truth hurts." "I'm sorry you misunderstood the joke." "I'm sorry you're so sensitive." Although these all include the phrase "I'm sorry," they come off as insincere and ultimately place the blame on the person receiving the apology.

A recent white paper published by Mount Holyoke College addressed the impact of insincere apologies. "Good apologies can prevent small problems from escalating and are a useful tool in conflict resolution... on the other hand, an insincere apology can make matters worse. Most people can sense when someone is being insincere and they may become even more offended than they initially were. When people feel that they have been wronged and fail to receive the apology they deserve, they often continue to feel hurt and resentful and are more likely to seek revenge or punishment."[9]

There are six kinds of non-apology apologies—and none of them benefit the one who thinks they are apologizing.

1. **"It's Regretful That...."** It's so often used because it doesn't require you to admit you did anything wrong. You're just sorry it happened...

2. **"It Seems That Errors Occurred."** The ultimate non-apology, acknowledging that something bad happened, but implying that you didn't have anything to do with it. It also has the benefit of not pointing the finger at anybody.

3. **Apology Directed at Another Issue or Person.** "I'm sorry you misunderstood my intent." "I'm sorry I live in a country where politics is so polarizing." "I'm sorry my uncle acted like such a fool." You really aren't sorry; you're just mad.

4. **Apology Used as Emphasis to Make a Point.** "I'm sorry, but that show was awful!" Why do you have to say you're sorry? You didn't write or direct the show. Maybe you're anticipating that they liked the show, so you don't feel bad about potentially disagreeing with time. Either way, it's disingenuous.

5. **Apologies in Advance.** "I'm sorry if this offends anyone, but...." "I'm sorry if there's anyone here who likes Barry Manilow, but...." You know someone is going to be offended, but this way, you can say what you want with a clear conscience. After all, you did apologize up-front!

6. **Deflective Apologies.** When Lehman Brothers went south, then-CEO Richard Fuld said, "I have been doing a lot of

soul searching...I will never heal from this."[10] Note that he said nothing about being sorry for any corporate blunders or malfeasance on his part for over-leveraging his firm.

All of these manipulations use the format of the apology to perform a completely different function than expressing sorrow for one's action, apologizing, and asking forgiveness. What they all do is make you appear dishonest and, dare I say it, sleazy.

Though there is no universal standard to determine when an apology is truly warranted, the following should be taken into consideration. When we wrong someone we know, even unintentionally, we are generally expected to apologize. It's that simple. Acknowledging injury and accepting responsibility for causing an injury allows us to meet the expectation of others. You don't apologize with the expectation of receiving an apology in return, you don't apologize when your intentions have been misinterpreted, you don't apologize as a ploy to get out of arguing, you don't apologize for everyday behaviors (coughing, sneezing, yawning, slipping), and you don't apologize as a way to blame someone else.

Everyone who has worked at Johnson & Johnson in the last 35 years points to the clearest example of successfully taking responsibility for a huge mishap without going through a major apology scenario. When Tylenol had to be pulled from the shelves due to product tampering, management said the company would do whatever it took to prevent it from ever happening again. They changed the capsules to gel caps and devised tamper-evident/resistant packaging. Six months after Tylenol returned to the stores, they recaptured 81 percent of their market share. Not only was J&J dealing with a powerful brand, but they didn't erode it with a hand-wringing apology. The lesson here is that, in business, the best apology is taking responsibility.

Unnecessary and/or non-apology apologies can erode your credibility, honesty, and leadership. They can make you look weak, vulnerable, and mendacious. In sum, they can seriously erode your brand. Think very carefully next time you're about to say, "I'm sorry." Are you really sorry, or are you something else?

? Test Yourself!

1.	What are the four most damaging words to utter at the beginning of any presentation?
2.	How could over-sharing potentially damage your brand?
3.	According to psychotherapist Beverly Engel why do women over-apologize more than men?
4.	Why might women have a lower threshold than men when determining what requires an apology?

Test Yourself! (continued)

5.	What is a non-apology apology? Give six examples.
6.	What should be taken into consideration when deciding whether or not an apology is in order?
7.	What are the dangers of unnecessary or non-apology apologies?

Chapter 5

Say What You Mean: Not What You Think They Want to Hear

Even if you are a minority of one, the truth is the truth.
—Mahatma Gandhi[1]

Mission Statement
The truth may sting but it always cleanses.

In a world dominated by "political correctness" (or fear of unemployment), we often feel compelled to sugarcoat or back-pedal our thoughts and ideas. After all, it's much more important to our comfort zone to avoid rejection or the possibility of "offending" someone than to put ourselves out there. Here's the thing: If you don't put yourself out there, you won't be rejected, but you won't be accepted either. Successful personal brand impact depends on one's ability to take appropriate and clear stands that will allow you to distinguish yourself and, above all, demonstrate value. Watered-down thoughts will make you instantly forgettable—we like people who have opinions, and if you want to stand out and be memorable, it's imperative that you communicate honestly as well as politely.

We live in a culture that frowns on dissent and prizes agreement. Our body language may indicate agreement—we may be silent or deliver a tepid "yes"—when on the inside, we are in complete disagreement. Regardless of the relationship (friend, colleague, family member), most of us prefer to smooth over differences rather than be confrontational. We also value speed over deliberation, and feel that it's important to get our work done as quickly as possible to preserve relationships and avoid conflict.

This is in direct opposition to the notion that growth and innovation are dependent upon a certain amount of "constructive tension." In my previous book, *Be the Brand*, I discussed the importance of taking mere informing to persuading and getting people to act during any conversation. There's always a certain amount of conflict when trying to persuade someone to do, think, or act differently, and if we avoid these temporary moments of discord, then very little gets accomplished.

> "It is discouraging how many people are shocked by
> honesty and how few by deceit."
>
> —Noel Coward[2]

The truth is that bosses, for the most part, don't like a lot of dissent and do not foster a culture of communicating differences, despite the heralding of a corporate "speak-up" culture. What is often fostered is an environment where loyalty is measured by how much one accepts corporate decrees and policies—with only superficial challenges. If we want to hold on to our jobs and move up in our organizations, stifling conflict is the safest way to do it, or so we believe.

And, lying to avoid conflict in the office is quite common, according to Carol Kinsey Goman, author of the new book *The Truth About Lies in the Workplace*. She conducted a survey of business professionals which found that 53 percent admitted to lying to cover up job performance issues or as a means of career advancement.[3]

I can't tell you how many companies I visit that herald a "speak-up" culture, but really don't advance the notion of sharing or expressing differences. On the contrary, it's common to see a more "top-down" culture where employees are considered loyal if they tow the company line, values, and decisions with minor dissent. I think it's safe to say that as a result of the signals sent by corporate hierarchies, if they want to advance, or even keep their job, avoiding conflict is the less risky avenue.

And although it's appropriate to point the finger at bosses, they are not the only ones who raise the fear of dissent. Our brand is on display for everyone, with potential consumers everywhere, and our concern about our image extends to subordinates and peers alike. We can be rejected or scorned by them as well, so we don't want to risk creating a negative impression or cause a potentially embarrassing incident.

The problem with this is stifling conflict often elevates the odds of the negative impact we fear the most—that is, work streams taking longer to perform tasks, sometimes unsuccessfully. Also, when key issues are not properly vetted due to unexpressed conflict, it can potentially ruin and/or devalue good relationships.

Every time we crush conflict, it sets a more concrete precedent: that it's good to be silent. The downward spiral continues, and although we may think that it makes relationships relatively safe, the conflict doesn't go away. It gets suppressed, and the work suffers. We feel less satisfied and less engaged. Potential disaster looms around the corner as a result.

Not being constructively honest (dissent with a viable alternative/solution) cuts across all organizations, regardless of size, influence, industry, or location. And when the economy goes south, it gets worse because everyone is worried about possibly losing their job—so, creating a pseudo-"kumbaya" atmosphere is preferred over dealing with simmering differences and/or disagreements.

It is really quite simple: Say what you mean and mean what you say. The ramifications for not doing this could be dire, especially in business. The potential for wasted time and effort as a result of poor/ineffective communication is considerable, along with the additional collateral damage of anger and frustration. In fact, a career can be significantly derailed when you are unclear, are disingenuous, or contradict yourself.

Then there are those who are afraid to say what they mean because they don't want to potentially turn off the individual to whom they are speaking. I have known many individuals in sales who value maintaining client relationships over inserting constructive tension to change behaviors (that is, get their clients to buy more), and their year-end numbers reflect this. Or, to avoid conflict, they say nothing (when they should say something) and completely erode their credibility. Remember: It's business, not a social relationship. You can't forget that. (They certainly won't.)

> "If you ever injected truth into politics you have no politics."
>
> —Will Rogers[4]

Probably the most famous and successful "truth teller" of the 20th century was humorist and entertainer Will Rogers. Born in Indian Territory in Oklahoma, this humble Cherokee turned cowboy turned vaudevillian became one of the most famous and listened-to people in the world simply because he "told it as he saw it." He became such an iconic figure that at the time of his death, *The New York Times* devoted 13 pages of coverage. President Franklin D. Roosevelt said, "His appeal went straight to the heart of the nation. Above all things, in a time grown too solemn and somber he brought his countrymen back to a sense of proportion."[5]

And probably, the major reason he was so successful is because he never attacked people personally—but told the truth about behaviors and actions of which he disapproved (or approved). For example, he famously denounced the stealing during the Harding administration (remember studying the "Teapot Dome scandal"?), but did not attack the individuals who were eventually sent to prison for their misdeeds. He focused on the culture in Washington at the time. During Theodore Roosevelt's administration, the Native American Five Tribes experienced the greatest treaty abrogation, yet he kept his attacks aimed at the thievery that was occurring, not the man in the White House. The same thing happened when he criticized the government during Hoover's administration as being pro-business and anti-people (especially the poor). He took on Washington without having to belittle the president. Everyone listened to him and, above all, believed him!

The lesson here is that you can hold people accountable without playing the blame game. Our fear around truth telling often centers on the negative reaction we might expect from those to whom we deliver feedback.

However, as Will Rogers proved, if you deal with the situation ("we have a problem with retention, as the culture of this department doesn't go out of its way to express appreciation for people's efforts") as opposed to attacking the individual ("if you made appreciating people's efforts more of a priority, you'd be able to retain people") you'd get the action needed while taking the fear out of the equation. This kind of strategic facilitation is critical, especially in high-performing organizations in which egos are strong and associates are constantly jockeying for position.

Much more recently, Andy Rooney, the late (and much missed) cantankerous pundit of *60 Minutes* was a regular fixture on Sunday night television. We all waited to see what sacred cow he was going to eviscerate next. No matter whom or what he talked about, we believed him, because he always told the truth and was truly an "equal opportunity offender." Unlike the predictable positioning of the pundits on many of the network and cable news outlets, you never knew what Mr. Rooney was going to target and what he would say, but regardless, he always made sense. When nouvelle cuisine was all the rage at fancy restaurants (carefully arranged bits of food at sky high prices), Mr. Rooney famously cracked, "I don't like food that's too carefully arranged; it makes me think that the chef is spending too much time arranging and not enough time cooking. If I wanted a picture I'd buy a painting."[6] When online purchasing began to take hold and consumers began to wonder about the extra fees they were being charged, he declared, "I understand shipping—you have to expect to pay for the stamps or for the freight company—but what's this handling they always have? How much does handling cost, anyway? I don't want a lot of people handling something I'm going to buy before I get it."[7] Who could argue with that?

Being known and respected as a truth teller (and always being believed) is a huge asset in any community, business, or organization, just as not being trusted or believed is a career-killer. So, here's a plan to help you say what you mean:

Ask yourself what you would say if you weren't worried about being right or about the reaction, then edit your words to make them more tolerable and specific.

How liberating it would be if we could always say exactly what we wanted to, without a filter or worrying about being judged or reacted to in a negative way. Unfortunately, real life doesn't work that way, but that doesn't mean we have to avoid issues altogether or be afraid to express our true opinions. Once you've figured out what you would say if you weren't worried about being right, or concerned with the reaction you would get, then adjust the language to what you think your audience can handle. I've tried this many times, and I've discovered that people have a much higher tolerance for constructive tension than you think. The first few times, lean on the conservative side, then as you get more comfortable with this approach, you can begin to take greater risks. And remember, these should be benefit-driven conversations as well. If you accompany your thoughts with the benefits your audience would accrue if they saw things "your way," you'd be amazed how they would gloss over the things you feel would be difficult for them to hear, and focus on what they'd get out of it. Here's an example:

Real Thought: HR is always talking about work-life balance, but they're full of it. If I didn't put in 10 hours a day and be willing to work on weekends, I'd never get everything done, and my job would be in jeopardy. What hypocrites!

Audience: Staff meeting with manager present.

Adjusted Language: While I've heard a great deal about the importance of work-life balance, I'm having great difficulty integrating it on a day-to-day basis. It would be extremely worthwhile for us to look at our work load to see if there's a way to effectively manage expectations about what can reasonably be accomplished during a typical workday. I think that would also have a beneficial effect on retention in this department.

You have to ask yourself what result you are seeking when you speak up and edit your words, targeting them toward the result you want. I have always subscribed to the notion that awareness without solutions is useless.

As soon as I hear someone ask me, "Do you mind if I share an observation with you?" I immediately tell them, "As long as you tell me how to fix whatever you've observed. Don't make me aware of some deficiency if you can't help me solve it." So, in the process of saying what you mean, be sure you have a good idea of the outcome. In short, it's perfectly okay to vent, but be sure you have a plan to go with it. And make sure your words reflect what your audience is going to get out of it.

Edit your words for blame and emotional reaction

Editing your words is critical! One of the most powerful motivators of behavior is shame, or what we'll do to avoid it (almost anything). No one is going to want to listen to you if you play the blame game aimed at people inside or outside the room. The idea is to safely express your thoughts and drive action to a desirable outcome. It doesn't do any good to preface comments with, "If it weren't for XYZ, then this wouldn't be happening," or "They don't have a clue how this is going to roll out." You always want to deal with the situation, not the person(s). As opposed to "They don't have a clue..." try "While the prevailing wisdom is that we've anticipated all contingencies, the achievement of a seamless roll-out may be more complex than we originally anticipated. We need to look at...." Notice the use of "we" in order to avoid finger-pointing. This will make your comments inclusive ("one for all and all for one") as well as much less threatening.

Say what you mean and mean what you say

While flexing new "speak-up muscles," you might find that defensiveness comes out as a mean voice ("Now that I've liberated myself to speak up, you're going to be the recipient of my pent-up frustration").

Instead of letting it speak for you and potentially misrepresent your brand, express yourself in a more strategic and thought-out manner that can turn a negative message into one that could be interpreted as complimentary and positive. For example:

- ➲ "You know, you can really be annoying sometimes" can be changed to "It's amazing how confident you come off sometimes."

⮞ "I can't believe how bossy you can be" becomes "You're always so clear about what you want and need."

⮞ "You always have to be right" turns into "I appreciate how concerned you are about me falling on my face, but sometimes you need to let me experience that painful face plant."

See how this works?

You can also try using the "deposit before withdrawal" style of criticism instead of just going in for the kill and criticizing. Begin by complimenting something (the deposit), accrue some equity, then constructively criticize so you can end with the benefit to them if they modify their behavior ("You have great style, and in a business setting, a more conservative approach might have people listening more to what you have to say as opposed to focusing on your look. It all depends on what you want people to take away."). Basically, you want to speak to others as you would like others to speak to you.

Our level of self-esteem is largely based on our ability to feel that we have a place at the table and are being heard—that we have some input into what goes on in our life and are not merely being reactive all the time. When we can't say what we mean, the consequences can be dire; we feel "less than" (inferior), as well as frustrated. Conversely, when we are able to be honest and constructively transparent, we feel we matter, what we think matters, and our words matter. To clearly and honestly communicate one's ideas, thoughts and needs is a key skill toward building valuable relationships. First, it tells people what you want, and it can prevent you from being taken advantage of. Regardless of cultural conditioning (personal and professional), standing up for yourself is critical.

Robert C. Roberts of Baylor University and W. Jay Wood of Wheaton College wrote in their book, *Intellectual Virtues: An Essay in Regulative Epistemology*, about how we need to face the challenges around us with honesty and intellectual integrity. The authors divide intellectual virtue into six categories.[8] The three that resonated most with me are firmness, humility, and autonomy. Regarding firmness, on the one hand, you want to avoid being the individual who caves on beliefs when initially confronted or opposed, though you don't need to be stubborn and maintain your position against all evidence to the contrary. The virtue of firmness seeks a middle ground. A person with firmness can evaluate and add new information on top of a solid foundation and is able to ratchet up or down the intensity of his or her beliefs based upon the quality of the new information. Roberts and Wood contend that firmness and mental agility are directly related.

Humility is a critical component of intellectual virtue. Does your desire for status interfere with your objective view of what you perceive to be the truth? The truly humble individual avoids such vanity and need for self-aggrandizement, placing concern for others ahead of oneself. Intellectual virtue, which includes humility, allows you to learn from others at any point in time and to avoid becoming overly arrogant.

The virtue of autonomy guides you down a path of individualism but avoids unnecessary conflict with authority and tradition. Never blindly adopt whatever your boss or someone else tells you. However, failure to accept guidance from those who have more wisdom or helpful information may come at your peril. Tradition and authority have their place, and the person who has mastered this virtue knows when to accept it and when to be an individual.

Being able to stand up for yourself and always say what you mean will not always get you what you want. However, the chances of getting at least some part of what you want are greatly enhanced by your ability to articulate what you mean. Also, even if your argument (with constructive tension) doesn't carry the day, at the very least you can gain comfort in knowing your voice was heard!

? Test Yourself!

1.	Give several reasons why we often don't say what we really mean.

Test Yourself! (continued)

2.	How does the focus on maintaining relationships conflict with innovation and growth?
3.	What is constructive tension? Why is it important?
4.	Explain "saying what you want to say in a way others can hear it."
5.	Why is awareness without solutions a problem?
6.	How do we counteract "mean speak"?
7.	What does it mean to "make a deposit before you make a withdrawal?"
8.	What is the importance of feeling you have a voice?

Chapter 6

Sharing Is for Sissies: Directing
Desired Outcomes

*Wisdom that a wise man attempts to share always sounds
like foolishness to someone else.*

—Herman Hesse[1]

Mission Statement
An impactful plan of action motivates people to do something;
sharing makes it optional!

My mother (as well as most everyone else's mother) told me that it's
important to share. Sharing was a sign of breeding, generosity, and inclusion. Being an obedient child, I followed my mother's instruction, and even
expanded my sharing portfolio: I would share to get people to like me.

Clearly, I was not the only one to adopt the concept of sharing as a
platform to ingratiate. In the business world, I hear time and time again,
especially during presentations, "I am here to share with you the results
of the great work we are doing on..." or, "I would like to share with you
the figures on...." It seems that everyone wants to share, but in reality they
want much more, and are too ingenuous to be transparent.

Case in point: Being a working mom who travels a great deal, I missed
many of my child's typical "mommy/daughter" experiences, and by the age

of six, Avery was really beginning to resent my absences. Clearly, I had to do something, so I decided to kill many birds with one stone. Becoming a class trip chaperone at my daughter's school was a big deal and in a pool of parents angling for the prized role, I had prevailed. So, in addition to spending some quality time with her, I was going to show all those other parents how a real "super-mom" could perform. I was going to milk this for all the missed everythings for the previous two years and show stay-at-home moms that we working stiffs really could manage work-life "integration." I got to write the invitation letter detailing the purpose of the excursion, and set forth the rules of conduct, dress code, and snack. I purchased the orange T-shirts and collected the money, determined drop-off and pickup; this was my parental zenith. I counseled my six-year-old daughter on her role as my surrogate (peer leader). I had pretty much covered all the bases. One small problem, however; notice how none of the aforementioned details had any benefits to the kids or reference to fun— but no matter, I was on a mission.

The visit to the Bronx Zoo had gone better than expected. The buddy system worked—nobody got lost, no one had any accidents, everyone got a souvenir, and I smelled victory. That is until the moment on the bus ride home when I announced it was snack time. Many of the girls looked at me in dismay as they, in fact, had no snack. Their moms hadn't packed any! Score one for the business professionals! But the win was pyrrhic as reality set in. I was the class trip mom and I had failed them. Somehow, I should have foreseen this or at least reminded the other mothers. I had to salvage any success of the day, and although I couldn't save them all, I could make Avery an example of generosity. At least there might be an opportunity to demonstrate the spirit and benefits of giving (clearly my agenda, not my daughter's, I assure you). You see, *I* had packed a generous bag with an assortment of sweet, savory, and healthy treats. Though I couldn't feed the entire bus, I could at least provide for Avery's seat mates.

As discreetly as I could, I leaned forward and whispered to my progeny, "We need to share." She ignored me and began foraging in her bag. I announced my directive again and then finally took her to the back of the bus. "I'm not kidding. You need to share," at which point she returned to her seat and offered her bag to the little girl to her left, who helped herself

Part II

Reinvention Tension
(Rewarded)

to a considerable amount. Avery then handed her bag to the little girl on her right, who took the remainder and handed back the empty bag to my daughter. If looks could kill!

We continued the rest of the trip in silence. When we arrived back at the parking lot, Avery waited until every other child had filed off the bus. She then skated by me, turned around, and said, "You made me share, they ate all of my snack, I'm hungry, and they don't like me better! Are you happy?" She turned and left me inhaling bus fumes while I ruminated on the overall failure of the experience. *"So, Johnny, tell our loser about today's consolation prize!"*

Don't get me wrong—this is not a plea for selfish and stingy behavior. I'm a big believer in being gracious. However, when you share, that should be its total intent and outcome: to redistribute an imbalance of something (assets, possessions, food). But more often than not, we share not to redistribute, but really drive some sort of collateral action (feel a certain way, do something a certain way, regard the "sharer" a certain way). And in this ADHD world we live in, this use of the term *share* is disingenuous, passive, and ineffective. If you want people to listen and appreciate you, take your advice and follow your direction; then the transparent approach is always the way to go. State up-front the benefits (to them) of what you're about to discuss and why they should care. This will prompt the action you want them to take, or at the very least, strongly consider your desired outcome. The term *sharing* makes it optional, *sharing* makes you passive, and *sharing* masks your true intent.

I would be most remiss if I did not digress here and bring up an alarming trend that has been fueled by the extensive number of social media platforms. Facebook, Twitter, Instagram, LinkedIn, Pinterest, Tumblr, Google Plus+, VK, and Flickr are all designed to make it simple for us to share anything and everything with everyone—immediately! I find it fascinating that so many people feel the need to reach out to their cyber-friends with endless useless information 24/7. Besides the potential for privacy violations (including the sharer and anyone else mentioned in the various posts) this constant stream of blather has become intrusive and completely distorted the term *share*, turning it into something sophomoric and pedestrian. There's just too much sharing going on with no apparent desired outcome, which makes the use of the term almost dangerous these days. It's critical to understand this whenever trying to inform, persuade, and get people to act on your information.

So why do we do all of this sharing? What does it get us? Not as much as you think.

- ➲ **Sharing as code/cover for "do this!"** Bosses, parents, friends—they all use the *share* word when imparting advice, information, and directives when all they really want is for you to do as you're told. "I'm pleased to share the new POA for the coming fiscal year," says the vice president of sales, when all he really means is "I'm telling you what I expect you to do in the coming year." "Honey, let me share something with you: Your hair is really getting too long," says Mom. What she's actually saying is "Get a haircut." "Let me share an observation with you: Gina (the current girlfriend) doesn't bring out the best in you," says the best friend. Translation: "Dump her!" We think that by using the word *share*, we make it optional and less threatening. We see through this every time and it makes you seem weak and manipulative. Try the direct approach. It may not always get you what you want, but you'll always be respected when you speak.

- ➲ **Sharing to impress.** This generally comes under the heading of "I know something interesting that you don't, which makes me powerful." The latest corporate shake-up, who's hooking up with whom, someone's inappropriate compensation, a review of a "hot ticket" show, an impending divorce—with baited breath, the keeper of such "scoop" imparts, "I have dirt to share!" No, they're not really sharing; they're trying to show you how well-connected they are because they possess juicy information. Beware of those who tell you they're sharing, when really they're trying to "one-up" you. I see this all the time on

Facebook. I do not find this sort of sharing impressive. Quite the contrary, it makes we want to avoid the person when I see them coming at me.

During corporate business presentations, results are shared to either impress the audience (generally management) with performance, or warn them that performance has gone over a cliff. But this isn't really sharing, is it? It's delivering information for a very specific purpose, and you risk trivializing your information by sharing (as opposed to impressing or warning).

➲ **Sharing to re-assign blame.** This is one of the more insidious uses of the term in the share lexicon. "Let me share with you what really happened." What they really mean to say is "It's time for me to correct the record." Much more impactful, don't you think? In this case, sharing allows you to merely be the messenger and take no responsibility (the ultimate passive-aggressive strategy), whereas correcting the record is a proactive, transparent, and more honest approach. The former is weak; the latter reflects strength and the willingness to take some risk. How would you rather be perceived?

➲ **Sharing to shift responsibility.** I hear this all the time. "We need to share the various tasks in order to ensure a timely roll-out." Apparently, before they were shared, the owner realized they couldn't accomplish what they needed to on their own. Oops! How about "It appears that the original distribution of tasks has proven to be unrealistic, given our deadlines. We need to shift some things around in order to get this done on time."

➲ **Sharing to soften bad news.** This is often used at large meetings ("The time has come to share our plans for the upcoming reorganization"), less-than-favorable annual reviews ("I need to share some observations with you"), a negative prognosis ("Let me share with you the latest test results"), being passed over for a job ("I'd like to share the thinking of the search committee"). You see where I'm going with this? The mere substitution of the word *share* with more transparent terms such as *discuss, deliver,* or *review* would make those statements much stronger and honest.

In *Be the Brand*, I discussed, in detail, the ubiquitous use of minimizers during oral and written communications such as *just, briefly, kinda/sorta, hopefully,* and *l'il bit,* in an attempt to ingratiate ourselves with our audiences, which serves to make us and what we have to say insignificant. I am now going to add "share" to the list. I'm not saying you should never use these words, just like there are times when sharing is absolutely appropriate. But for the most part, as I did with my daughter, the concept of sharing is used to falsely ingratiate or take us off guard. The honest truth is that in this very self-centered society in which we live, left to our own devices, we would tend not to share, or do it under very special circumstances (with people we truly care about for truly altruistic reasons). Clearly, this has changed dramatically, and it needs to stop!

Moving forward, think twice before you say the word *share*. Other, more suitable, honest choices are: *discuss, talk about, deliver, give, promote, detail, de-mystify, communicate, drive,* and *shift*. Note that these terms are much more specific and require a particular course of action; sharing is extremely generic. As you shop your brand, it's imperative that you remain unique and under no circumstance should you default to anything that resembles generic.

If I had to do it all over again, I should have let Avery have her snack while the other girls watched. It wouldn't have hurt their relationship and you can bet that the next time those girls went on a field trip, they would make sure their mothers packed a snack—and that's a lesson worth sharing!

? Test Yourself!

1.	Why do our mothers tell us it's important to share? Does it work?
2.	How have you heard the term *share* used during business presentations?
3.	When is sharing or use of the term *share* appropriate?
4.	Name three kinds of "sharing" that disguise a different intent.

Test Yourself! (continued)

5.	How has *share* become a minimizer?
6.	How has social media affected the use and meaning of the term *share*?
7.	What are the dangers of inappropriate use of "sharing"?
8.	Name six words that can be used instead of *share* to greater effect.

Part II

Reinvention Tension
(Rewarded)

Chapter 7

Vent With a Purpose

Never tell your problems to anyone... 20% don't care and the other 80% are glad you have them.

—Lou Holtz[1]

Mission Statement
Don't taste the "whine."

In the 2006 movie classic *The Devil Wears Prada*, most audience members sympathized with the put-upon young fashion assistant, Andy Sachs (Anne Hathaway), and hated the magazine's demanding editor-in-chief, Miranda Priestley (Meryl Streep). I didn't! As a boss, I'd hired too many Andys and could relate to the film's illuminating dialogue between Andy and her immediate supervisor:

Andy: She hates me, Nigel.

Nigel: And that's my problem because...oh wait. No, it's not my problem.

Andy: I don't know what else I can do because if I do something right, it's unacknowledged. She doesn't even say thank you. But if I do something wrong, she is vicious.

Nigel: So quit.

Andy: What?

Nigel: Quit.

Andy: Quit?

Nigel: I can get another girl to take your job in five minutes...one who really wants it.

Andy: No, I don't want to quit. That's not fair. But, I, you know, I'm just saying that I would just like a little credit...for the fact that I'm killing myself trying.

Nigel: Andy, be serious. You are not trying. You are whining. What is it you want me to say, "Poor you, Miranda's picking on you. Poor you. Poor Andy? Hmm? Wake up. She's just doing her job.[2]

When you re-run the tape, Andy's not so sympathetic is she? As Maya Angelou wrote in *Wouldn't Take Nothing for My Journey Now*, "What you're supposed to do when you don't like a thing is change it. If you can't change it, change the way you think about it. Don't complain."[3] Call it a pivot or epiphany, my moment of truth came shortly after I'd made what I thought was the life-changing decision to leave corporate America to become "my own boss" as president (secretary, bookkeeper, and janitor) of a fledging consulting firm. I gave myself the title of founder and CEO, and was feeling quite superior. I would now be calling the shots. Well, that feeling lasted for about two weeks before I realized that with no team or department reporting to me, I had to personally show up at an important product launch meeting. The decision was agonizing; it meant I would miss my daughter's first ballet recital. I wasn't so in control after all. About three days later, still hung over with guilt and resentment, I went to meet a former colleague, now client, who had just put me on a large retainer. We had always been close, so when he invited me into his C-Suite office, motioned to the overstuffed sofa and said, "How's my new favorite consultant? Sit down, take a load off, tell me how's it going." I thought he cared, so I did. "Well you know, I'm still grappling with that work/life balance thing. I thought as a consultant I'd have more personal time, but I missed my daughter's dance recital last weekend." Suddenly, Ted jumped from his seat and made a "T" sign with his fingers. "Too much information," he snapped. "As a consultant, I pay you to be perfect. As president, this company pays me to be perfect. People watch me getting out of my car in the morning. They read my body language, am I having a good day or a bad day. Should they be concerned? So every day as I walk through the front door I say to myself, 'It's Showtime,' and I put on my game face. Now Tamara, you know I love you, but as a consultant I pay you to be perfect. I honestly can't worry about you or your career choice. So next time I ask you, 'How's it going?'—you smile and you say, 'Fine'."

I was shocked; I left defeated and cried all the way home. I couldn't wait to tell my husband. Surely he would understand how cold this response was; he would support me and express the proper sympathy. "Best business advice you ever got," he responded. "Just exactly what did you want Ted to do with this information? You've just learned two important things: Negative TMI makes people recoil, and bosses don't need more awareness. They need solutions!" As Ted went on to say, "Don't be the messenger of bad news. Don't bring me a problem, personal or professional, that you aren't prepared to own and solve."

Ted was telling me I had to do my own intervention. Stop complaining to the wrong people, making others feel guilty about my situation, my choice, my lot in life. While I was no longer hiring "Andys" as a solo practitioner, I was channeling them. I had become an unhappy employee, subordinating my priorities to the cruel dictates of an unreasonable boss—me! I had uncorked the "whine" and was drinking liberally from the bottle. Light-bulb moment: It was clear I couldn't be in two places at the same time. I had to clone another me. That meant recruiting, training, and hiring staff and paying them with income the business didn't have. Did I want to limp along, unable to balance personal and professional commitments, because I had no ability to say no to clients when life got in the way? I decided to change my business model and be a team instead of an icon. I took out a loan and built my brand.

It was amazing how right that decision turned out to be. Word spread that TJC, Inc. could handle large and small assignments, that we had greater availability, and could even take on simultaneous assignments. Confidence among my clients grew and I was soon booking enough business to repay the money I had borrowed. Clients shared with me that though they wanted to sign on in the past, they had been afraid; if something happened to me how would they maintain the relationship and how could I guarantee the deliverables?

Fast forward 20 years. Having enthusiastically embraced the concept of not tasting the whine, I was now teaching it (very successfully, I might add) as a sought-after executive coach. My mantra is my mission, and I seal every contract by telling clients that "developing your voice, realizing your potential" is more than a tagline—it's our guarantee. But occasionally there are exceptions to every rule. Take the case of Stephanie. On paper, she is a winner in all ways: attractive, Ivy League grad, an MA *and* MBA from a top-tier school, and an enviable professional track record of increasing responsibility. What could possibly need fixing? Apparently her attitude. As the famous expression goes, "Attitude is everything." Stephanie had been more than "tasting the whine"; she was drunk on it. At first it was fairly subtle, not finding time on her calendar for us to meet, not returning the pre-meeting questionnaire. I had been cautioned by Stephanie's boss that she was on the bubble. Dubbed as passive aggressive and on the watch list because of her lack of support for that same boss who now viewed her as "talented but a limited contributor." Willing to give Stephanie a "proof period," Margaret had brought me in as an executive coach to turn her around or she'd give the green light for HR to turn her loose.

Weeks after our original meeting was supposed to take place (Stephanie rescheduled twice) we met in her office. After a tepid smile and an unenthusiastic handshake, Stephanie informed me that someone had told her I was in her office the previous week using her phone to dial into a conference call. "No big deal," she said, "only it would have been nice if someone cleared it with me." We both laughed—she a little malicious, me a little nervous. I was already on the defensive. "Well your secretary said it was okay—that you were gone for a week and wouldn't mind." I was "on notice." That set the tone for the next 90 minutes.

"No worries, I know how to do this," I thought. Disarm her; put some deposits in her ego bank. I told her what a great first impression she made—that her professional look was impeccable. Stephanie accepted the compliment and ran with it, telling me how she took great pride in her appearance and how it was always noted, for good or for bad, that sometimes being so fashionable and business appropriate made her colleagues uncomfortable because they couldn't meet her standards. Oops—some whine was starting to tip out.

Then I talked about the feedback Margaret had given me on Stephanie's work product, always getting the job done. "Yes," she replied, "but I'm more of an administrator in this role. I process the projects. It's not rewarding. I want to manage people. I'm working beneath my title. The last person in this job was incompetent and they reduced his responsibilities, so now I'm left in the narrow lane he created. Nobody is recognizing my real contributions." The plot thickened.

I knew the department was about to conduct their year-end review assessments, so I asked Stephanie to share with me her list of accomplishments (contributions). She handed me an official piece of paper listing all her "activities" for the past 11 months. I was a little taken aback. Everything was very literal—a time line full of "whats" with no connection to "whys" (benefits to the department or the company). I told her she had not connected actively to outcomes. She needed to "declare vs. "share"— advocate for her initiatives with the positive changes they provoked. This seemed to surprise her and she took note, vowing to change her approach. This is how she would get recognized, rewarded, and promoted. For good measure, I also told her to smile more—that she looked a little "scary." She said it was due to lack of sleep and that she was generally much more cheery.

Thinking I'd made some significant inroads, I took this information back to Margaret, who informed me the jury was still out. In fact, she had almost cancelled my contract, believing Stephanie could not be redeemed after all. At a department meeting the previous week, Stephanie had apparently been drinking from the "whine fire hose." Turns out she'd gotten the same feedback from her supervisors that I had given her. Declare versus share, be animated, "sell" the benefits of her work, smile more, and so on. But instead of being positive, she had gone negative. In front of senior management Stephanie went on a tear about the lack of secretarial support, long hours, and no direct report responsibilities. Clearly she was there to vent versus solve. The reaction from the franchise head was predictable; they were all expected to do more with less. So exactly what was Stephanie's point? At that moment, though Margaret had lobbied for Stephanie to be given a second chance (at least a second look based on her job performance), attitude trumped achievements and Stephanie's "meets expectation" rating was calibrated down.

With this assessment, management knew she would be a flight risk, but frankly no one cared. The question was: Would Stephanie learn from the feedback, stop playing the blame game, and have an attitude adjustment? The answer ultimately was no. Though I continued to try to course correct with her, Stephanie resented and resisted the intervention. She left the organization three months later, and with no references and recommendations is still finding a "better fit."

As I discussed in my previous book, *Be the Brand*, everyone perceives what they see, hear, and experience through the lens of vested self-interest. What Stephanie perceived as justified entitlements was looked at as self-indulgent behaviors by her peers and superiors alike. She was so inward facing that she couldn't understand why her needs, with constant complaining, weren't being met. She also overestimated her value, which was a critical error. You know the old expression "The squeaky wheel gets the grease"? Well, in this case, the squeaky wheel got replaced.

So where does venting/complaining have a rightful place? When you are able to call out a problem, turn it into an opportunity, and provide a solution.

Following my stint at a major public relations agency, I was brought in-house as vice president of communications for a large, international healthcare company. Barry, the man who hired me, was the president, and he became a quasi-mentor to me. It turned out that I was one of the highest ranking women in the company, which had, up until then, been a very male-driven environment. I didn't realize it at the time, but insecurities crept in and I found myself dropping Barry's name into conversations in order to ensure that my points were being heard. "Well, as you know,

Barry wants to..." or, "I was speaking to Barry this morning, and he feels that...," or, "I was with Barry at a conference yesterday, and he said..." This strategy worked for a while, but my honeymoon period was soon cut short. During one of my "Barry inserts," a brand director asked to have a sidebar with me. "When are you going to stop dropping Barry's name into everything you say?" she ranted. "People around here are starting to think you're having an affair with the boss, and they're starting not to like you. I'm sure you have very good ideas and thoughts that are independent of Barry—for god's sake—use them and stop coming off like Barry's puppet!" Although this woman didn't report to me, I clearly outranked her, yet she felt strongly enough about this to pull me aside and castigate me for my "Barry Strategy." I was initially miffed, but then, the more I thought about it, the more I realized that she was spot on. Regardless of what I thought, I was being perceived as Barry's mouthpiece, which was getting me nowhere. From then on, I couched my comments as my own and found that I began to get traction. As my credibility grew, I felt more comfortable taking creative risks and soon developed a strong fan base. I evolved from presidential stooge to major contributor to strong leader. And this might not have happened had this brave woman not taken the bull by the horns and called me out. She could have just talked behind my back and complained about me (as I assume others were doing), but felt confident enough to vent and give me a plan of action. As a result, I used her as a sounding board for many of the projects I was involved in and was instrumental in securing a major promotion for her. We are friends to this day, and I continue to recommend her for jobs while she helps me with my business development. Now that's what I call venting with a purpose!

Years ago, I was marooned in Montreal en route to St. John's in Halifax. There was a bad snowstorm and getting flights out of Dorval Airport was near impossible. As it was around the Christmas holiday, you can imagine the complaining and whining going on between the stranded passengers and the ticket agents. It was critical that I get to St. John's; though my client would understand a delay, I had to get there by the next day at the latest. So I got in the very long customer service line and spent an hour listening to angry passengers yelling at the airline personnel. One by one they were told there was nothing that could be done for them and they'd have to wait. I thought, "This is not working. I'm going to try another tack." So, when I finally got in front of the agent, I smiled and laughed, "Happy holidays!" She laughed, too, and we were off. I asked her if she got "battle pay" for days like this, and she rolled her eyes and replied that it was just part of the job. I said that I was in the service business too and really sympathized with her plight. I then told her that I certainly had no intention of adding to her pain and was merely inquiring what the situation was. After she said quietly, "Well, no one is getting out of here tonight, that's for sure," I queried, "Well, you're obviously a smart lady—if you were me, what would you do?" She answered that because she knew the country well, she'd have no problem renting a car and driving in the storm, but she wouldn't recommend that to me." I thanked her and said I appreciated her kindness as well as her patience with the unruly mob. She then paused and quietly told me, "Hold on a minute. I have one seat on a fight to Toronto first thing tomorrow morning, where you can connect to St. John's, and be there before lunch. Does that work?" I was thrilled. Out of the hundreds of people at the airport, I was one of the very few who was given a ticket out of the snowy hell of Montreal. She went even further to make sure I got a decent room at one of the airport hotels. I got a restful night's sleep, woke up, had flowers sent to that helpful agent, and got on my way. Wouldn't you know that down the road she became a very successful travel consultant, whom I have used extensively because of her access to the best deals. Talk about getting more flies with honey.

We all have been subjected to bad tables at restaurants, lousy hotel rooms, and really uncomfortable seating on planes. But what do most people do about it? They fume and yell and, more often than not, get little satisfaction. Whenever I am given a poor table at a restaurant, I simply tell the manager, "You run a wonderful establishment here and not only do I want to keep coming back, but I would also like to recommend this to my friends and colleagues. Do you think you could find me a table that is not next to the air conditioner or the kitchen? I would really appreciate it." It's amazing how, when employing this technique, "We have no free tables" becomes "Right this way."

I travel 30 to 40 percent of the time for business, so my hotel experience and a good night's sleep mean a great deal to me (and the focus of my keynotes if I arrive at meetings well rested). I share my needs and my expectations with the front desk when I check in and, as a result, you'd be surprised how often I get a free upgrade. Then I do what most guests do not: I fill out the comment card, compliment by name all the people who have made my stay so enjoyable (from valets to porters to the concierge), and I leave a thank-you note with the hotel manager. Because this act is so rare, it sets me apart and makes me memorable. When I return, I am usually welcomed back enthusiastically and given VIP accommodations (even at such five-star hotels as the Langham in London and the Mandarin in NYC).

You can take this to the bank: Nobody likes to hear complaints unless they are accompanied by solutions and the benefits to following those solutions. It's really that simple. The next time you feel the need to vent, put yourself in the position of the one listening to the diatribe. How would you react? Chances are you'd do everything you could to cut short the conversation and avoid that person for the foreseeable future. But if you can say, "I have a problem with this, but I also have a solution that will drive a better outcome," not only will you be listened to, but you will gain tremendous respect and credibility.

Here's a blueprint for constructive venting with a purpose:

- Make "ego deposits" before you critique. Tell them what's right, good, or working—then you have the equity to make a "withdrawal."

- Explain the problem and what they can do to fix it.

- Once you give the solution, tell them what's in it for them if they follow your advice (the all-important benefits).

- Everybody likes a problem-solver; nobody likes a complainer. And as everyone knows, too much whine leads to bad hangovers.

? Test Yourself!

1.	What's the difference between someone "picking on you" and someone who is just doing their job?
2.	Why is it important not to air problems without solutions?
3.	What are some of the pitfalls from playing the "blame game"?
4.	When is venting appropriate?
5.	What are the benefits of being "outward facing" as opposed to "inward facing"?
6.	What is an "ego deposit" and why should you always start with one?
7.	How does putting yourself in the *role of receivership* help when you need to vent?
8.	What is meant by "venting with a purpose"?

Chapter 8

Assertive, Not Aggressive: Nobody Likes a Bitch

We despise and abhor the bully, the brawler, the oppressor, whether in private or public life, but we despise no less the coward.

—Theodore Roosevelt[1]

Mission Statement
You get more flies with honey than you do with vinegar.

Let's face it: Nobody likes a bully, and no matter how powerful one thinks he or she is, what goes around comes around. I am reminded of the infamous "Chainsaw Al" Dunlap, a "corporate decimator-for-hire" who was brought into one financially ailing company after another to "rescue" their operations, when all he really did was apply a fanatic focus on the companies' numbers, sacrificing everything else. His slash-and-burn tactics when he ran the appliance giant Sunbeam finally became his undoing. First, he fired as many people as possible. Then, at an investors' meeting, his tactics around advancing sales dates for products (ahead of delivery) in order to improve his quarterly sales numbers were brought into question. Following the meeting (attended by many Wall Street big shots) Dunlap grabbed one of the more vocal critics, shoved his hand over the man's mouth and, as reported by *BusinessWeek*, screamed, "You son of a bitch. If you want to come after me, I'll come after you twice as hard."[2] His tactics were finally viewed as violating accounting practices and he was fired. Unfortunately, Sunbeam was unable to rid itself of the taint of "Chainsaw Al" and filed for bankruptcy a few years later. Oops!

We could fill many books with stories about corporate sociopaths at all levels (and genders). Many psychologists have built large followings trying to explain the deep-seated dysfunctions that cause such behaviors. But here's the simple truth: Bullying, or overly aggressive behavior, is not leadership; it's just bullying. I'm sure you've heard the old expression "Leaders have followers, managers have subordinates." So, if you think that the best leader is the loudest, think again. If, in your office, you rule by fear, know that you're never going to hear the truth from anyone. You'll just hear what they think you want to hear, because they're afraid.

Leadership is all about engagement and the ability to effectively persuade, not intimidate or dominate. Too often, managers and team leaders resort to intimidation, bullying tactics, and other forms of negative interaction with their colleagues and staff to move their agenda forward. However, their actions are more counter-productive and counter-intuitive than their negative behavior would ever justify.

Aggressive behavior in the workplace and the toll (physical and mental) that it takes on both managers and other senior executives can be long-lasting if not devastating. In a study authored by the National Science Foundation for the U.S. Department of Veterans Affairs, "the top 10 aggressive behaviors identified in the workplace include:

1. Being treated in a rude and/or disrespectful manner.
2. Not given the praise for which you felt entitled.
3. Glared at in a hostile manner.
4. Delayed actions by others on matters that were important to you.
5. Given little or no feedback about your performance.
6. Given the *silent treatment*.

7. Not given critical information that you need.

8. Being lied to.

9. Prevented from expressing yourself.

10. Someone interfered with your work activities.[3]

Any of this sound familiar? In each of the previous examples there are nuances and intensity differences that make the aggressive affront track on a scale between one and 10. However, no matter whether the affront is a one or a 10 (or anything in between), there is no substitute for appropriate, affirming behavior in the workplace that can bring the team together and not pull them apart. An interesting *Forbes* study noted that people rarely leave their jobs for more money, but many quit because of a bad supervisor.

Doesn't it make sense that overly aggressive behavior won't get most of us recognized, rewarded, *or* promoted? In business situations, it's a sure bet that the domineering, loud (occasionally screaming), "winner take all," "I'm right and you're an idiot" types, even if successful in the short-term, will not have an extended life with any organization or beneficial long-term relationships with external partners. Further, the more debilitating and hostile a situation, the more a company—through inaction or inattention—has exposed itself to civil lawsuits and government penalties and sanctions by watchdog groups like OSHA and the ACLU.

Years ago, a very good friend of mine was a senior associate at a high-powered New York law firm. He worked in the real estate department and, at the time, the head of that business was a man I'll call Howard. Now, I know that corporate real estate is a tough business, but Howard re-defined tough. My friend reported that during team meetings, if things didn't go Howard's way, he'd shriek at subordinates, "What are you doing? You're freaking killing me!" His screaming matches were legendary—especially at the frequent around-the-clock negotiation sessions when he would threaten bodily harm to anyone around him. Yes, he made a lot of money for the firm, but his political capital was not limitless.

One evening, Howard sat down in front of his television and at the age of 52, suffered a massive heart attack and died on his couch. Two days later, there was a huge funeral at Riverside Chapel, and outside, on the sidewalk, immediately after the service, all of Howard's partners were dividing up his clients. No remorse, no sadness. My friend told me that he'd rather die in the poorhouse than go out like that. Howard wasn't a leader; he was Mussolini in a suit.

Nobody who's worked with me would ever say I was a wilting flower. I'm convinced that one of the main reasons for any of the success I've enjoyed is my relentless assertiveness. In business, you have to be, because if you're not, there's someone right behind you who's ready to take over.

However, because we are advocating on behalf of acting assertively over being aggressive, let me be very clear: Asserting yourself doesn't have to mean that you dominate others, just like being passionate doesn't mean that you have to come across as out of control or threatening. You can be an advocate for your ideas and thoughts while being open and available to seek input from others. Bombastic speakers who bully during conversations usually turn people off and push them away. Their overzealous, negative, strong-arm tactics have no long-term upside. In the short term, needlessly aggressive managers may get their way. But, in the long term, colleagues and coworkers will go out of their way to avoid engaging them; so what did they "win"?

In a recent *Nightline* interview, Sheryl Sandberg, COO of Facebook and author of perhaps the most successful business book in the past few years, *Lean In: Woman, Work and the Will to Lead,* said, "Leadership is not bullying and leadership is not aggression. Leadership is the expectation that you can use your voice for good. That you can make the world a better place."[4]

I don't know when it happened, but somewhere along the line, successful assertion has turned into a scorched earth domination tactic—*I win; you lose.* Well, the truth is that in most cases, the most notable exception being the practice of law/litigation (as my friend's boss, the late Howard, embodied to perfection), if everyone doesn't win something, everyone loses.

Jack Welch, former CEO of GE, was asked in a Harvard Business Review feature about what makes an effective manager. His reply was, "Good business leaders create a vision, articulate the vision, passionately own the vision, and relentlessly drive it to completion. Above all else, though, good leaders are open...they don't stick to the established channels. They're straight with people. They make a religion out of being accessible."[5]

Many managers are too stuck in their negative behaviors to be as open or as accessible as Jack Welch suggests. To eliminate their aggressive styles, perhaps even to give up what's worked for them in the past, including bullying tactics, would mean admitting defeat. Sadly, while the alternative (assertive behavior) is much healthier and more inclined to help the organization than the kind of aggressive tactics we now see all too often, sometimes it's a struggle to convince the offender that *assertive* trumps *aggressive*. What a bully doesn't understand is that when you communicate and intimidate with fear, people avoid you and you become more isolated. And operating in isolation is a sure-fire formula for failure, *especially* in business.

David Marcus, one of the new generation business titans, and the president of PayPal, says, "People will only change the way they do everyday tasks if it's overwhelmingly clear how it makes their lives better."[6]

Being assertive but not aggressive can make a huge positive impact in the lives of everyone concerned. The business benefits are quantifiable and begin with improved moral. A better climate at the office can lead to an increase in sales, a more efficient operation, increased employee retention, and a streamlining of productivity across the board. A bullying or bombastic executive who can modify his or her behavior will most certainly generate more traction within their workforce. An employee who seeks to be assertive without being aggressive or passive stands a better chance of being recognized, rewarded, and promoted then if he or she continues to play the role of Attila the Hun or Mickey Milquetoast at the company holiday party.

> "Sometimes you have to be a bitch to get things done."
> —Madonna[7]

Madonna's statement is true, if "sometimes" refers to "the last resort." Richard Branson, chairman of the Virgin group, and by all accounts one of the world's most successful and *nicest* moguls, believes, "There are lots of ways to get your point across and make your business successful without being aggressive. Always remember that you love what you do and your role is to persuade others to love your business, too, and therefore, to want to work with you."[8]

What does it mean to be assertive and not aggressive? Being assertive doesn't mean carrying the biggest stick, or having the loudest mouth, or even making the best points; that's aggressive. According to Sue Hadfield and Gill Hasson, the authors of *How to Be Assertive in Any Situation,* "Assertiveness is an entirely different approach to meeting your needs. It's about letting others know what you do and don't want in a confident and direct way. Being assertive means you do not feel you have to prove anything, but neither do you think you have to allow yourself to be mistreated. You set boundaries and feel entitled to defend yourself from exploitation, attack and hostility."[9]

Being assertive is perhaps the best tactic I've found to defend against bullying behaviors at the office. There are a number of ways each of us can choose to communicate with our superiors, our subordinates, and our coworkers (some more effective than others).

Assertive

As we talked about in the previous passage, assertiveness is the most advanced, most effective way to communicate in a professional setting. Assertive people thrive in hard-to-define situations. Assertive people are able to come to their own defense and delineate healthy boundaries without being hurtful in the process. Being assertive means you are open to and value others' opinions, but you're also not willing to give your power away by agreeing too quickly or yielding to another's point of view too readily. You've found a healthy balance between sticking to your guns and allowing others to participate while not minimizing or disparaging another for the sake of proving a point. Being assertive is the best way to approach most situations while managing up, down, and sideways. Being assertive means you have nothing to prove but also are willing to set appropriate boundaries against belligerence, anger, and confrontation.

An interesting side note: According to insurance industry senior executive Robyn Farrell, "Being assertive can be difficult especially for women, even in these modern times. Many women have been taught to be agreeable, passive, and polite, to avoid conflict and to make those around them feel at ease—even submissive..."[10] and it seems to prevail, even when women reach the peak of their career.

Careful—this is a confusing case of "tone" versus "intent." I have the privilege of working with a dynamic female company president (let's call her Stacy). She is loved by her employees and direct reports, and she feels really good about being loved and really bad about hurting feelings. How refreshing in a corporate leader! But sometimes it gets her into trouble. In an effort not to offend, she frequently gives an unenthusiastic nod or a bland verbal acknowledgment. Unused to this genteel style of communication, people bring their own agendas to meetings with her, fail to "read" the real reaction, hear it the way they want to, and move forward only to be "roadblocked" later as the tension builds, the stakes get higher, and the "no" finally comes. They feel it's unexpected and unfair. And these interactions may take away from Stacy's positive standing. I have warned people to listen for the intent not the content, of Stacy's response. And I have counseled Stacy that she has enough equity to be more assertive and respond with a firm no versus a flimsy yes.

Aggressive

Aggressive behavior gives people permission to respond with counterproductive, insensitive, hugely demotivating, insulting responses in a wide range of situations. Generally, aggressive people talk over others, are unwilling to listen and respond with openness, will use any and all methods to gain an advantage, and view the world purely through their own narrow lens. Without behavior modification, overtly aggressive managers usually have a limited shelf life, as at one point or another they are likely to anger the wrong person. Being aggressive allows a singular viewpoint to be heard, but in the process creates a culture of alienation that cannot be undone.

Passive Aggressive

Being passive aggressive is aggressive behavior, but acted out in a more cowardly, indirect way. Passive-aggressive people often suppress their true feelings of anger and resentment by giving other people dirty looks, not returning phone calls, imparting misinformation, using sarcasm, and giving people the silent treatment. Essentially, passive-aggressive workers express their discontent non-verbally, through action. Calling in sick, complaining on message boards (anonymously), and habitually showing up late are others ways that passive-aggressive employees act out. Unfortunately, being passive aggressive is no way to get recognized, rewarded, or promoted, yet sometimes the negative benefits of this behavior are too strong to pass up.

Passive

Passive people tend to let everything go. They have no backbone and are unwilling to stand up for themselves in meaningful and appropriate ways. Passive people wish to avoid confrontation at all costs and generally have trepidation about coworkers' and superiors' responses to things. Passive people generally have a tough time getting in the middle of office politics. Even if they have a sense of good or bad, right or wrong, up or down, they are unwilling to speak their minds and stick their necks out. Essentially, passive people are not able to address issues of any kind, and are somehow content to let others do the heavy lifting. They are interested in keeping the peace at all costs, no matter if issues fester under their nose.

It is in the best interests of everyone in the workplace to strive for the healthiest communication skills possible. As Warren Buffett noted, "It takes twenty years to build a reputation and five minutes to ruin it. If you think about that, you'll do things differently."[11] No manager ever has an excuse to act like a bitch (male or female) or to treat an employee like his or her bitch ever again. It's not only counterproductive and potentially career ending, but organizations large and small are finding it harder and harder to excuse bad, aggressive behaviors even from talented earners.

The following ideas are a handful of suggestions I would urge you to consider when making the commitment to practice an assertive communication style. You can leave passive and passive-aggressive styles by the side of the road; there will never be a need to employ either of those techniques now, or in the foreseeable future.

Your reason to believe

Understand that you are contributing and bringing substantial worth to your team by doing everything you can to manage assertively, fairly, and without prejudice. You have every reason to believe your best interests and the best interests of your organization are served when you choose an assertive, not aggressive style. In so doing, you will engender a magnetic, positive response from your team—one that could contribute materially to you being recognized, rewarded, and promoted.

Keep emotions in check

Aggressive managers tend to be reactive and off-kilter. If you're angry, count to 10 and don't act on your frustration. You will marginalize and limit your ability to flourish if you lose the ability to keep your emotions in check. If it's too tough to hang in, grab a coffee and take a walk. Five minutes might be a huge game-changer when it comes to managing your emotions and others' responses.

Set clear boundaries

Often it's hard to separate personal from professional, friend from frenemy, and employee from friend. The more you can keep yourself free from emotional attachment, the more you can act assertively with no harm, no foul. Although it's true that having a vested interest in the outcome of any management decision is important, it's also clear that staying neutral and open is essential if you're to manage assertively with balance and impartiality. Understand the difference between grabbing a drink or two with a colleague after a long, tough day and telling things to that same employee that are inappropriate or can compromise your ability to act in a balanced and professional manner.

Pick your fights wisely

From time to time, you might have to take a step closer to an aggressive style. If that's the case, never give yourself permission to make it personal or hurtful. Stick with the issues, stay forceful, and don't back down. Being assertive doesn't mean you have to be anyone's bitch. Nor does it mean you have to be a bitch to win the battles, which do rage from time to time.

Another reason to choose positive, assertive behaviors over negative, aggressive ones is health related. According to a study done at the National Institute of Occupational Health in Copenhagen, the results of bullying, teasing, and violence in the workplace can have a lasting negative impact on mental and physical health.

The study of aggression in the workplace found that bullying victims exhibited "more short-term depressive symptoms and mental health problems..." among other stress and emotional problems and "a lower physiological stress response was found in the non-bullied employees." In addition, "more short and long-term fatigue and mental health problems" were reported in victims of nasty teasing while those who were victims of violence "reported short-term stress reactions and more long-term symptoms of fatigue...."[12]

Life is not about winning a continual popularity contest. Tough decisions have to be made all the time. But how many successful leaders do you know who are unpopular? Not many, I'll bet. If you demonstrate confidence (by being assertive) and, as a result, I feel you're going to lead me in the right direction, I'll follow you anywhere.

？ Test Yourself!

1.	Why don't aggressive managers get the truth from their subordinates?
2.	An N.S.F. study listed 10 manifestations of aggressive workplace behavior. Give three examples.
3.	According to author and Facebook COO Sheryl Sandberg leadership is devoid of what two qualities?

Test Yourself! (continued)

4.	What does former GE CEO Jack Welch say makes a good business leader?
5.	Name the four primary communication styles.
6.	Name one characteristic for each of the four predominate communication styles.
7.	What are the dangers of unchecked aggression and violence in the workplace?

Chapter 9

What Goes Around, Comes Around

I'm a true believer in karma. You get what you give, whether it's bad or good.

—Sandra Bullock[1]

Mission Statement
Bridges should be built, not burned!

In my business, I've had the good fortune to secure many long-term clients. Throughout the years, with the help of my team, organizations have grown and prospered, and the individuals we've coached have been promoted and often gone on to greater glory. Every now and then, however, a "tenured" client will tell us that they want to take a break, for whatever reason. Often they feel that after all this time they've got it covered. Frankly, our goal is for our clients to evolve their messaging, branding, presentation, and strategic communication skills to the point at which they can fly on their own; that's what I call a success.

One of our long-term clients was using us to, among other things, message and coach presenters for their annual national sales meeting. Our original agreement called on us to work with the main tent speakers on their presentation content and flow, and rehearse them on-site at the meeting. As it often happens, our scope of work increased as the project went on; we were asked to work with the brand teams and training department as well as the main tent speakers. In addition, we were asked to conduct a separate workshop for part of the sales team. Once it was clear we were working way beyond our original agreement, I put in a request for additional fees to cover the extra work. This request was slowly moving up the approval chain as we headed toward the meeting site in Orlando.

The executive who hired us had been a client for many years and had worked at this company for most of his adult life, rising from being a sales representative to district manager, to national sales director, to vice president of sales. As others came and went in the organization, Mark (as we'll call him) stayed and advanced his career. He always told us we made significant contributions to the company and championed our involvement in many areas.

As the big meeting approached, we had been privy to some discreet but consistently negative comments about Mark and how he was handling certain people and business activities. I found this odd, as his dealings with us had always been positive as well as productive. The complaining reached such a point that the training director told us that he could barely stand to look at Mark in recent days.

We were having our own concerns, as a signed copy of the request for additional fees had not been sent to us, even though I had been told that this would not be a problem. The day before the end of the national meeting in Orlando (when we had basically completed our work), I called the client's home office to inquire about the fee approval. I happened to get Mark's administrator, who told me that it had been approved, but at the last minute, Mark pulled it. She assumed that he had already spoken to us about it. I thanked her and got off the phone fuming. We had done the work, and now, after the fact, Mark was questioning our fees.

I sent him an urgent voicemail demanding to speak to him. He got back to me that he was in the middle of conducting employee evaluations. "How can you bother me with this now when I'm dealing with people's careers and livelihood?" I responded, "Because your actions have directly affected my career and livelihood, Mark." At any rate, we did meet a short time later, and he was as cold as ice. He felt I had no right not only to confront him on his actions, but also to confront him at his meeting, where he had so many more important things to deal with. I wouldn't let him off the hook. I said that after all the years I had been in business, I had never been treated in this manner, especially given our track record of outstanding collaboration and work. After going back and forth, he realized he was fighting a losing battle (especially because I wasn't supposed to find out about him pulling our agreement for payment until *after* I returned home from the meeting), and begrudgingly agreed to pay us the agreed-upon fee.

At the conclusion of the meeting "debrief" back at the home office, we were told that moving forward, they would handle their communication needs internally and wouldn't require our services. As I mentioned at the beginning of the chapter, this happens on occasion. But I knew that their internal capabilities were non-existent and Mark was basically firing us because I stood up to him. Well, my eyes were finally opened regarding Mark and I realized that we would, most likely, never work with that company again.

Fast-forward two years when I ran into Mark unexpectedly at an industry function. He was very cordial and said it had been too long, that their presentations at meetings were awful, that he'd like to talk to us about maybe coming back, and then he began to ask me if I knew about any opportunities outside his company. He was asking me about helping him find a new job! Not much later, I found out he had left the company and, after looking unsuccessfully for a corporate job, was starting his own consulting business that competed directly with mine. And he had the nerve to ask me for an endorsement on LinkedIn. I got a call from his former training director who asked, "Did you see Mark's listing in LinkedIn? He actually asked me to endorse him as well. I'm not only 'not endorsing' him, I'm telling everyone I know to stay away from him!" Between us, we know at least half the people in the industry. Not a smart series of moves, Mark.

If my experience was an example, clearly Mark thought he was secure enough in his position that he could treat anybody as he pleased with no significant consequence. Only when he felt his job was in jeopardy did he reach out and try to make nice before he asked me to help him find a new job. But by then, the bridge had been irreparably burned. I really don't know how well his consulting business is doing, but I do know that it could be doing a lot better with my active endorsement.

No matter how far you may have progressed in your career, it's critical to stay on good terms with superiors, subordinates, and peers alike. You never know when you may run into them again and need to be in their good graces.

By building bridges, we basically mean building relationships. In a recent edition of *Fast Company*, best-selling author and business leadership guru Ken Blanchard reported that "...a major telecommunications company commissioned some research to find out which attributes best predicted long-term leadership success. Why did some leaders succeed while others never really lived up to expectations? After examining a variety of factors—including tenacity, intelligence, work ethic, ingenuity—they discovered that the ability to build and leverage a network of relationships was the best predictor of success."[2] Had Mark understood the value of managing his relationships successfully, he probably wouldn't have gotten such negative pushback when he hung out his shingle.

Mr. Blanchard went on to say that "building collaborative work relationships is a challenge for many people. Relationship building is generally not taught in schools and it's rarely taught to those who join the managerial ranks."[3] Considering the critical nature of relationships as a driver of success, I would consider that a huge issue.

Regardless of the industry or field you are in, teamwork and commitment toward a desired outcome are essentials for success. Yes, a single individual can make a significant impact, but part of your role, as a leader, is to ensure that together, your team can take on much greater outcomes than you could as individuals.

A critical by-product of building bridges is evolving your career—transitioning from executor/contributor to manager/leader. This requires that you help others reach their goals and objectives in order for you to reach your goals as well. How is this done? Basically, you have to change your thinking from you and what you want to do, to focusing more on the team you wish to lead. What are your team members trying to accomplish? How can you facilitate their needs? Through that lens, you will be helping to ensure that your company's objectives are being met as well as the team's.

In Chapter 7, I discussed the hapless Stephanie who was so concerned with her own needs that she forgot she was part of a team. Even after I was brought in as a form of "intervention," she still shot herself in the foot and burned every bridge in sight, despite her immediate boss's desire to give her the benefit of the doubt. Her inability to appropriately manage up, down, and around amounted to career suicide (at least at that company).

As a leader, it's important that you are able to communicate a definitive vision, how your team can help realize the vision, and how the results will benefit everyone as well as the company. Again, you want to be perceived as a unifier (as opposed to a negative force—looking to find fault) as well as a person who can drive action.

Here are some tips that can help you keep your bridges secure:

1. **Build psychic equity before debt.** Effective relationships with colleagues are driven by mutually beneficial exchanges. In order to make sure these exchanges happen almost automatically, it's important to create equity in a person's psychic account that you can draw from when things occasionally hit a rough patch (which happens all the time). Once you have built an emotional reserve, you can withdraw as needed.

2. **Be egalitarian as opposed to opportunistic.** We see this all the time. Some individuals only go after building relations with people they think are high on the totem pole and can benefit them while, at the same time, ignoring those who are lower on the food chain. What happens is that relations with peers and superiors are fine, but those down the line (that is, subordinates) are unhappy and generally disgruntled. As someone who is supposed to lead, you need to be effective at managing up, horizontally, and down, simultaneously.

3. **Building relationships is key in any professional situation.** Don't fall into the trap of feeling that reaching out to

colleagues is somehow "selling out"—that you are above that sort of thing, and that all the company needs are your skills and brain power, that somehow your "work speaks for itself" and engenders confidence and respect. This is dead wrong. Success in any endeavor is about building good and appropriate relationships—in one's personal and professional life. No one operates well in a vacuum, and isolating yourself puts you in one.

A very successful CEO, Lenny, whom I knew earlier in his career when he was a training manager, was very strategic regarding his bridge-building. He worked for a very successful operating company of a large, multi-national organization in which access to the executive team was relatively limited. He found out that the senior vice president usually began his day at the company gym, around 6 a.m. Armed with this information, Lenny made it his business to also be in the gym before sunrise in order to engage with the SVP on an informal (but very exclusive) level. As their relationship grew, so did Lenny's career at the organization.

4. **Relationships should extend cross-functionally.** A common error people make is to create a circle of relationships that include only individuals who are like them or whom they perceive as peers. Successful leaders make sure they extend their circle to colleagues who are very different and possess varying skills/methodologies and work in other areas, at other levels.

A suggested way to build this circle of beneficial relationships is to map out what I call your Sphere of Influence, previously mentioned in Chapter 3. Simply take a piece of paper and, putting yourself in the center of a circle, connect to a series of spokes that are the key individuals you currently are (or should be) connecting to (superiors, peers, subordinates, internal, and external customers). Then, assess each of the relationships by determining:

- ➲ What is critical to each of them.
- ➲ In your function, if you are contributing to meeting their critical needs.
- ➲ The status of your relationship (good, bad, neutral).

If your relationship is neutral or negative, you need to figure out what the ramifications will be if it gets worse. Could it put you in jeopardy?

Ask yourself: *When is the last time I communicated with this person (directly)? Do I need to reach out more to keep the bridge "secure"?*

By creating, refreshing, and acting on your Sphere of Influence, you will be in a much better position to leverage these relationships moving forward. As you make your way up the ladder in any company, it's critical that you manage and nurture those beneficial relationships that you've built. We all spend a great deal of time at our jobs, and we want to work with people we respect as well as like. I have found that the individuals who are able to leverage these ongoing relationships by helping to ensure collective successes are those who are tapped for leadership positions. We discuss the all-important interview later in this book, but I will say now that the main purpose of any interview is not to discuss your skills and qualifications. They know those already and that's what got you the interview in the first place. All they basically want to know is if they would like to spend at least eight hours a day with you, every day. The importance of liking (respecting) those with whom you work cannot be overstated.

Whatever you do, don't minimize the importance of maintaining mutually beneficial relationships at work. You might feel that putting your head down and plowing through your work solo will avoid the traps of potentially toxic office relationships. However, this will severely curtail your potential to rise within any company and have any significant impact. In addition, being overly competitive with a "winner take all," or "my way or the highway" (hey, it's just business) will surely come back to haunt you.

Another individual I've known (and worked with) was the CEO of the company at which Mark, our bridge-burner, was employed. Louis, as we'll call him, was as charming as he could be but, in reality, the charm was skin deep, exceeded by real cunning and a win-at-all-costs attitude. A good friend and colleague of mine, whom I'll call Carol, went to work for Louis as president of his U.S. division. All was going smoothly until Louis asked Carol to sign off on some activities that she felt could be construed as unethical. She wouldn't go along. Louis and the owners of the company conspired together and soon, without any warning or notice, Carol was walked out of the building. They didn't even give her time to clean out her desk; her personal property would be sent to her. Carol was humiliated and realized how ruthless Louis had been. Eventually, the owners soured on Louis as well, and he was asked to seek new opportunities. Carol, in the meantime, was appointed as North American head of a growing health-care company. Soon, we were reading that Louis too had landed well and had been named president and CEO of another healthcare organization. Both of these appointments were not unusual, but what happened next was. The company Louis ran negotiated an agreement with the company that employed Carol to commercialize a particular product, but not in North America (Carol's territory). Given Carol's company's familiarity with the product landscape, especially in the United States, it's interesting that Louis passed on working with the U.S. organization. I have to think that had Louis not handled Carol so badly, he could have added North America to the agreement, thus making it a much more valuable transaction. Another burned bridge getting in the way of further success.

I understand there are times when circumstances prevent a "Hallmark" experience at the office. There's a great deal of stress, tempers flare, and the blame game ensues. That's typical. However, the gutting of relationships is often completely avoidable, and even though you may work in a large industry, it's a small world, and you can't afford to turn off too many people. You never know when you'll cross paths again.

I often work on projects that deal with multiple external vendors who supply a variety of services. Sometimes, our services overlap and there are occasional "territorial" issues. Several years ago, I was working on a large national sales meeting for a very important client. We interfaced with another external partner in a variety of areas, and sure enough we began to clash. Now, I thought I was fairly friendly with this organization, but they began to exclude me from meetings, didn't communicate critical information, and basically attempted to marginalize my involvement. I didn't take kindly to this, and even contemplated reporting and complaining about them to the client. That might have provided a temporary fix, but with detrimental long-term consequences. You see, in this arena, we constantly run into each other all the time, and a battle between us would come to no good down the road. So taking the bull by the horns, I invited my colleagues to lunch (on my dime) and reassured them that I had no interest in doing what they did, and assumed that they felt the same about me. Once we got the issue on the table, we were able to discuss better SOPs and how we could productively work together going forward. As a result, we now recommend each other to potential clients and have given each other substantial business.

In a recent article, Michael Hess of *Moneywatch* echoes my sentiments about groups with whom you should never burn your bridges: "Every good businessperson knows the importance of building quality relationships. But I'm surprised at how often people don't give the same thought to the 'quality' with which those relationships end, and the possible ways in which a bad breakup can come back to haunt them."[4]

To avoid burning bridges, think about the following groups and your relationship to each:

- ➲ **Colleagues (peers, subordinates, superiors).** It's a small world, as the saying goes, and if someone stays in the same line of work, chances are you will hear from them again, even after they leave your company. Maybe you'll even be working with them again in some capacity (whether you stay in your current position or move to another company). These people may take on positions that directly affect you in a big way, and your previous relationship will go a long way to determining your ability to be successful moving forward. So, when it's time to move on, for whatever reason, I strongly urge everyone to leave on good terms. And if you have to fire someone, make sure you do it appropriately and professionally; he or she may come back in your life as your boss later on.

- **Clients.** The need to cultivate these relationships is clear. But you can't please all the people all the time, and sometimes clients move on. However, in this world of immediate and pervasive communication, their potential comments about you could dramatically enhance or negatively affect your business. Make sure you continue to stoke those relationships even after the ties are severed.

- **Purveyors.** It's very simple: though there are multiple vendors for any single product or service, a shortage, special request, or time-sensitive situation could cause you to require a favor. You don't want to cut off a vendor when there is any possibility, down the road, you might need them. This could significantly impact your standing in your organization (and not in a good way).

- **Salespeople.** Most organizations that provide products and services use a sales force (sometimes referred to as account executives). And although reps may come and go, if they stay in the same industry, they probably have more contact with your customers (both potential and existing) than you do. A bad relationship with these "feet on the street" could come back to haunt you, especially if they leave your company to work for a competitor. Movement from one company to another is inevitable (and becoming more and more common these days). So you don't want to exacerbate a situation by being negative when a sales associate departs for another organization.

- **Competitors.** This is a subtle and nuanced series of relationships. Cordial relations with competitors are beneficial for a variety of reasons. You may serve together on trade associations or work on industry projects together. You also may hear about opportunities at other companies, which could be very beneficial to you. I am extremely competitive and certainly like to win, but having a vindictive and/ or snarky attitude toward those who work for competing organizations takes you down while you're attempting to tear them down. It makes you look small and may have big and negative outcomes in a world that is increasingly hyper connected.

As I stated earlier, business situations are not always the "Good Ship Lollipop," and occasionally relationships end acrimoniously. However, this should be minimized. As the title of this chapter says, "What goes around, comes around," and you never know when a bad split could come back to bite you at a bad time in a bad way. As the popular saying goes, "karma's a bitch."

? Test Yourself!

1.	What's the difference between someone "picking on you" and someone who is just doing their job?
2.	Why is it important not to air problems without solutions?
3.	What are some of the pitfalls from playing the "blame game"?

Test Yourself! (continued)

4.	When is venting appropriate?
5.	What are the benefits of being "outward facing" as opposed to "inward facing"?
6.	What is an "ego deposit" and why should you always start with one?
7.	How does putting yourself in the *"Role of Receivership"* help when you need to vent?
8.	What is meant by venting with a purpose?

Chapter 10

Don't Be Invisible: You Never Get More Than You Ask For

When I was young I thought that money was the most important thing in life: now that I am old I know that it is.

—Oscar Wilde[1]

Mission Statement
Let go of fear and negotiate from a position of strength.

A well-known television journalist recounted a salary negotiation session she had with a major network several years ago. When her potential boss made his first offer, she felt it was insultingly low. She countered with what she thought was a fair, competitive compensation rate and was told, "Oh no, you really don't want to do that. If anyone else finds out what you're making, they won't like you!" The journalist, instead of saying, "Who cares?" felt that the currency of being liked was more important than currency in the bank, so she capitulated and left a considerable amount of money on the table. Note that her qualifications or being appropriately paid was not brought up. Clearly, the savvy negotiator knew if he pushed the, "It's important to be liked" button (especially in the competitive world of TV journalism), he would likely force her to reconsider the position. The journalist minimized herself, as she didn't feel she was dealing from a position of strength. The good news here is that she realized she had been manipulated, so the next time she was in a salary negotiation, she stood her ground and actually got more than she expected.

A long-standing client of mine was in line for a significant promotion at a large healthcare company. When the head of his business unit left, he was asked to step in as acting head until a new leader could be hired. When this request was made, he was told that, though he was highly valued, he wasn't considered "ready" to hold the position on a permanent basis. Instead of devoting himself to changing that perception, his response was: "Oh, I understand. You'd have to be crazy to put me in this job permanently!" Predictably, he wasn't considered for the long-term assignment (and his fate was sealed!) and he was given a somewhat lesser promotion when the new head came in. When he told me this story, I asked him why he would devalue himself and take his candidacy out of the running. He replied that he didn't want management to think he was overreaching. "What's wrong with overreaching?" I asked him. "You're in marketing and sales—very competitive fields. How can you be effective without occasionally overreaching?" He had no response to that, but it was clear to everyone that although he held that job on a temporary basis, he was strictly a lame duck, which made his job even more difficult. His instinct was to be unnecessarily modest. As a result, his eventual promotion was unnecessarily modest.

Both of these anecdotes illustrate the difficulty many of us (even high-ranking executives) have with asking for what we feel we are worth. Asking for a raise, for more responsibility, to attend that Tuesday planning meeting, or to implement the efficiency program you've been working on takes self-confidence, guts, and a little bit of fearlessness. For most of us, expressing any kind of need is threatening—mostly because we fear hearing the word "no." There's something about "no" that instills fear and loathing in all of us. But if you think about it, "no" doesn't make us any worse off than it did before "the ask." Further, asking for what we want does not strictly communicate need; it communicates self-worth. Know this: If you don't ask for what you need or feel you're worth it, no one is going to give it to you. And if you don't ask for much—negotiating against yourself (Oh, they'll never pay me that...")—the impression is that you're not worth very much.

Let's face it: Rejection is a fact of life. Specifically, it's a part of everyday life. There is no way to avoid rejection completely. Overcoming the fear of rejection can be difficult, and it can take a lot of work to be okay with hearing the word "no." However, once you accept no as a necessary and regular occurrence, rejection becomes much easier to handle and actually provides clearer indications on how to proceed to yes.

According to Andrea Waltz, coauthor of *Go for No*, "You can achieve virtually anything you want—if you're willing to hear 'no' often enough." In addition, Waltz says that the majority of people inhabit a "Go for Yes" world and they will try everything "to get yes and avoid no. That leads to a mediocre life where you're always in your comfort zone." By staying in your comfort zone, you're missing the chance to be successful. Waltz concludes by saying "the no's are the stepping stones that get you [to the yeses]."[2]

When you negotiate on your own behalf and adapt your skills to handle almost any request you might want to make, also keep in mind there are differing opinions regarding whether or not directly asking for a raise is the right course of action for you to follow. It may surprise you that *only* asking for a pay raise might be poor advice for workers regardless of their gender (for example, high-paid female execs).

Victoria Medvec, the executive director at Northwestern University's Center for Executive Women, said in a panel discussion at Fortune Magazine's Most Powerful Women Summit, "You never ask for more money; you ask for more of a package. As you go into a negotiation, you always make it about what you are achieving for the business. The compensation should be the caboose of the offer. It is just along for the ride."[3]

When negotiating on behalf of your brand, you must always put yourself in the *"Role of Receivership"*: Am I giving value to those with whom I am interacting, or am I simply negotiating without understanding how my request is landing on the person with whom I'm negotiating?

Medvec concentrates her research on how decisions are made and the judgments used to arrive at these decisions. You are much more likely to get the outcome you want taking the *Role of Receivership* approach. "In a negotiation focus the offer on the other person and their needs," she says. "You also want to be flexible in your request. The best strategy is to think 'big picture' thereby allowing the conversation to include your total compensation package (all of which affects your bottom line) which might include travel, a car allowance, more weeks of vacation, expense account, lower deductibles on health insurance and more matching dollars for your retirement account."[4]

Highlighting and quantifying the benefits you bring to your organization are key components to a framing your negotiation. "Whenever I am in a place where I am thinking about myself and my pay, I am dead," says Christie Smith, a managing partner at Deloitte.[5] Instead, Ms. Smith always centers her negotiations on what problems she is solving for the business through her work. If you're able to take your manager through concrete examples of your performance, such as increased revenue, the development of new business models, improved efficiencies, and increased responsibilities, then a title change and pay increase might naturally follow.

This approach seems to have worked quite well for Mary Barra, the first female CEO of General Motors. Ms. Barra has been quoted as saying that she has never asked for an increase in pay—*ever*! Impressive, seeing as how she could earn as much as $14.4 million in her first full year on the job at GM if the Detroit automaker achieves certain goals.

According to Ms. Barra, she is motivated by her work and the value she is contributing. "I felt that if I did the right thing it would be recognized. I am not saying it is wrong to do (ask for a salary increase), in a specific situation. I just never faced that."[6]

With the focus of always adding value, it is no wonder that when *Time Magazine* was compiling 2014's annual list of the "100 Most Influential People in the World," Mary Barra was at the top of that distinguished heap. And in order to add value, clearly Ms. Barra had specific needs. The key here is that the needs were never perceived as personal. Whenever she wanted or needed something, it was always couched in terms of business benefits. Here's the problem with this for many of us: In addition to a fear of no, we also fear expressing need.

When I was growing up, my parents, when they couldn't, or wouldn't, agree to one of my requests, would reply, "What do you need that for?" or "That's ridiculous. You don't need that!" Pretty soon, I got the picture;

expressing any need would not only get a rejection, but also force me to question the need in the first place. Clearly, the "need" thing wasn't working. So, as soon as I was old enough, I began to earn my own money so I only had to ask them for things when it was absolutely necessary. Although it decreased the amount of conflict in my life, what I didn't realize at the time was that my avoidance of expressing need would cause problems later on in my professional life. It took me a while to re-train myself to ask for what I needed in order to advance the business and drive success.

Minimizing your needs and not asking for what you think you're worth is only a part of the challenge when negotiating on your own behalf. The bigger challenge: not broaching the subject in the first place.

Although gains have been made, there is still a gap between what women and men are paid for the same work. So, those studying this phenomenon are now zeroing in on the question not frequently asked: Why are women often reluctant to ask for more money?

According to economist Linda Babcock of Carnegie Mellon University, the average rate of pay for women is still $.78 to a man's $1.00. It gets worse, as she reports that the chances of a man asking for a raise in pay is four times that of a woman requesting a salary hike. Babcock goes on to say that the cumulative effect of this over time is huge. What happens is that even small raises lead to bigger annual salaries, which eventually lead to larger raises and bonuses. This hits home when you leave an organization and try to negotiate a larger salary with your new company. The thing they will always ask is what you are currently earning. Babckock says, "I tell my graduate students that by not negotiating their job at the beginning of their career, they're leaving anywhere between $1 million and $1.5 million on the table in lost earnings over their lifetime."[7]

Contributions to retirement aren't included in this lofty figure, which is generally based on salary level. Babcock goes on to say, "Women often just don't think of asking for more pay. If they do, they find the very notion of haggling intimidating, even scary." Instead, Babcock contends that women "wait to be offered" almost everything from an increase in salary to a promotion and even to be assigned to a specific project or team. Her conclusion is that since "those things don't happen very often," women are at a disadvantage versus men.[8]

It is a commonly held opinion that asking for what they feel they deserve is difficult for women. "'Part of the problem is that women are never taught how to effectively negotiate while avoiding being labeled as bossy or overly assertive,'"[9] observes Aimee Cohen, author of *Woman Up! Overcome the 7 Deadly Sins that Sabotage Your Success,* and an executive coach. Women also consistently minimize their accomplishments. Cohen continues by pointing out that if "you describe what you've done as 'no big deal' or say 'anyone could have done that'" it increases the difficulty in negotiating for more money. Cohen aptly notes that these phrases are seldom said by male negotiators.[10]

And the statistics for "minority" women are even worse than the pay gap statistics between men and women across the board. According to the Bureau of Labor Statistics, African-American and Hispanic women earn 68 and 59 cents respectively for every dollar a man earns. "At the current rate of progress," says a recent Department of Labor memo on pay transparency, "it will take until 2057 to close the wage gap."[11] This disparity became a rallying cry during Patricia Arquette's 2015 Oscar acceptance speech, where she emotionally declared, "To every woman who gave birth, to every taxpayer and citizen of this nation, we have fought for everybody else's equal rights. It's our time to have wage equality once and for all and equal rights for women in the United States of America,"[12] which was met with thunderous applause.

Now, although the pay gap between men and women remains, certain issues are gender neutral, and it revolves around that little word we referenced earlier: *no.* A factor that hampers negotiations for both men and women is an over-reliance on the word. It shouldn't be surprising that management's go-to response is *no.* Saying *no* maintains the status quo. Having a *no* response is often the easy way out. Senior executives and team leaders risk less when they say *no.* It means they haven't stuck their necks out or haven't gone to bat for someone or something, which could backfire if the *yes* somehow turns into trouble down the line. Saying *no* also has the effect of separating the weak from the strong. Typically the weak go away, and when the strong come back to the negotiating table, they often ask for less. When you think about it, it's not so much about "getting to *yes*" (the title of another popular business book) it's really about "getting past *no.*"

The ability to successfully negotiate something that *really* matters is a key leadership attribute. It combines verbal dexterity (the art of negotiation), with strategic evidence of accomplishment: increased productivity, higher sales, improved organizational integrity, and other obvious benefits that can be cited to help move a successful negotiation forward. You're usually in a much better position to begin a negotiation when the obvious benefits of your presence in the organization can be seen by those who have a vested interest in what happens to you.

As we've said before, everyone along the business food chain deals with important matters through the lens of vested self-interest, so you need to be realistic. If you're crushing your numbers, you have more ammunition to bring to the table than if you missed your sales forecast by 20 percent. But at the same time, never be afraid to request every bit of what you require, and then add some on top. You may raise expectations and have to produce at a higher level, but that, too, will be to your benefit.

When I was working as a corporate executive, I experienced a seemingly small but seminal event that changed everything. I was a member of the executive committee, and at one of our regular meetings I was assigned a project and told to report on my progress the following week. Feeling I didn't need any help (or not wanting to ask for any), I worked independently, and at the next meeting updated my peers, basically telling everyone that the project was completed and the problem solved. My boss asked to see me after the meeting. I was expecting a major pat on the back for a job well done, but instead was reprimanded. "No, Tamara, you weren't supposed to do the project yourself," my boss firmly told me. "We wanted you to gather input and report back to the group so we could make a collective decision. You're thinking like a consultant!"

Wow. What a revelation! That's what I was: a consultant! I needed to get things done efficiently, and not go through a protracted and multi-layered course of action in the process. Moving forward, this job was not going to fill that need for me. Two weeks later, I quit and set up shop as an independent consultant, and my former company became my first client. It was the smartest business decision I ever made! I was more confident to negotiate the right fees because it was easier to quantify my value, and

I was better equipped to have my needs met because they were all tied to advancing my newly minted "client's" business. Expressing and maximizing need became central to my success.

Most of us underestimate the power of asking. A recent study by Flynn and Lake brings the point home. They asked participants to get five other people to fill out a short five- to 10-minute questionnaire. They also asked the participants to predict how many other people they would have to ask to get five people to comply with their request. Most participants in the study overestimated the number of people they would have to ask. They predicted it would take twice as many as it actually took. In fact, to get five people to fill out the questionnaire, people had to ask about 10 people.[13] That's a hit rate of 50 percent—similar to the success rate of asking someone out on a blind date.

Asking is a powerful thing. According to a study by Annette Lareau, getting what you want may have more to do with attitude than aptitude. A privileged middle-class upbringing often leads individuals to feel like they deserve things and so they ask for them. As a result, their lives tend to be better than the lives of people who fail to ask questions. A sense of empowerment that leads you to ask questions is self-reinforcing. It tends to get you what you want.[14]

Perhaps more importantly, it sometimes gets you what you need. Malcolm Gladwell does an excellent job in *Outliers* of describing the perils of airplane pilots who fail to ask questions of their superiors and instead crash into mountains. Other recent studies have shown that students who fail to ask questions in classrooms are generally more worried about looking ignorant than they are about mastering the material. You can imagine the sad result of this.

Here's a simple, but rock solid truth: If you don't ask, you most likely won't get.

Most everyone (including the people with whom you work) is basically looking out for themselves (remember vested self-interest). But how come there are so many highly qualified individuals out there who are squeamish about advocating for themselves out of either fear or embarrassment? One reason is that some misguided souls believe that if they are truly deserving, good things will be offered without having to request them. As I stated earlier, only Cinderella had a fairy godmother. Even if management loves you, they rarely dole out largess, no matter how deserving, if it is not requested.

Here are foolproof strategies that can help you when you are negotiating key aspects of your professional life:

Define your anatomy of a W.I.N.

What Do I Want (What Do I Get?)

Intel Around Other Internal and External Candidates (What Do They Want/What Do They Get?)

Need to Identify/Commit to Resistance Points (What Are My Limits/What's Acceptable?)

Learn and Understand the "six steps before you sit."

1. **Preparation:** Know the facts. Know where the objections will come from.

2. **Set limits:** Determine how far you're willing to compromise.

3. **Keep emotional distance:** Feelings often cause us to make poor judgments and decisions. Keep them in check when negotiating. Remember: It's just business.

4. **Good listening skills:** Listen more than you speak.

5. **Clear communication:** Mean what you say, and say what you mean.

6. **Know how to close:** Understand how to end the conversation so everyone feels "whole" and you've effectively communicated your "ask."

When negotiating for what I want (and feel I desire) I call upon my "M.O.M."—an axiom I created to help me establish markers and boundaries—for a positive outcome versus soul-crushing compromise. Sometimes a "bird in the hand" leaves you holding a lot of "guano." So here it is, my position pillars: the **M**aximum I am seeking, the **O**kay I'll accept, and the **M**inimum I'm willing to take. Beyond that, walking away is the better win.

Consider the whole compensation package.

During a salary negotiation, when negotiating your total compensation number, remember to add things such as educational reimbursements, vacation time, sick days, car allowance, 401(k) matching funds contribution, and travel allowances into your negotiations. Do not get fixated on just getting more money. In the final analysis there are intangibles in your deal that will make your life better and save you a fortune in out-of-pocket expenses, which over time *will* correlate to more money in your pocket.

Go first!

Old-time negotiators say that it's smart to have the other side of the table make the first offer in order for you to make an appropriate response—in other words, be completely reactive. By making the offer first, you establish the baseline that will determine the entire arc of the conversation. *Business Insider* reports that those who go first with high offers usually wind up with a much higher final figure.[15]

Know Your *No's.*
No doesn't mean never (maybe just not now).

If you free yourself from the outcome of your negotiation, then you've let go of the shame associated with a *no*. You can't let *no* get you down, and you can't let *no* stop you. In many cases, *no* could mean something else—like not yet. In almost every case in which a *no* surfaces, look at it as a delayed *yes* and act accordingly. Be persistent, but don't be a pain. Keep after bosses (and clients) who've said *no*, and remember to stay professional.

A bad *yes* is worse than a solid *no*.

Where clients and colleagues are concerned, it's sometimes possible to use a *no* response as a way to deepen or strengthen the relationship. If you're willing to accept the idea that *no* isn't the worst news ever, then you can communicate that to peers and potential business partners, who might be uncomfortable saying *no*. You certainly don't want clients and colleagues to say *yes* if they mean *no*, and if you convey that you're willing to hear either answer, then a level of trust and ease will develop that could lead to many more *yes* responses down the line.

Learn from *no*.

While a *"no"* response isn't always desired, particularly when a raise or a big sale is in question, understanding why the response was a *no* is important to cultivating future success. Sometimes *no* is a sign of a performance issue that needs to be addressed. Other times it might arise from a disconnect with a client, such as a pricing or marketing concern that has been left unanswered. Whatever the reason, learning why a *no* response was given might just hold the key to getting a future *yes*, so don't take *no* personally and do whatever you can to turn today's *no* into tomorrow's *yes*.

It all comes down to having the confidence to determine what you're worth and asking for it. Rarely do we get *yes* the first time. But, like the saying goes, "It's not how you start, it's how you finish."

❓ Test Yourself!

1.	Especially in salary negotiations, why do most people have difficulty asking for what they think they are worth?
2.	What does the *Role of Receivership* have to do with successful negotiation?

Test Yourself! (continued)

3.	How can you demonstrate you "get them" when negotiating?
4.	What are the benefits of making the first offer?
5.	Why is it important to define the "no?"
6.	What can we learn from "no?"
7.	What is a "bad yes"?
8.	How can you practice before making the "ask"?

Part III

Edge *the* Ledge
(Promoted)

Chapter 11

Right Ladder, Wrong Wall

If the ladder is not leaning against the right wall, every step
we take just gets us to the wrong place faster.

—Stephen Covey[1]

Mission Statement
The search for work that feeds the mind and the soul is a
continual process that rests on the foundation of our life
experiences—both good and bad.

Though many of my friends know me through my work as a communication strategist and executive coach, they are unaware that I began my career on the stage. I studied classical singing and acting for many years and even toyed with the idea of going into opera (as you can imagine, I had a *big* voice). I entered competitions, sang in Europe, performed in summer stock—you name it. Finally, after all my hard work, I was cast in the national tour of a Broadway show!

Only devotees of obscure musicals would remember, *Do Patent Leather Shoes Really Reflect Up?* Based on a book by John Powers, it's a story that takes place at a Catholic school. I played a nun (remember: that's why they call it acting!). But a new director came in with his own vision. He recast the show, diluted the storyline, and left for the Great White Way with a flawed production. The critics agreed. To make a long story short, only five performances into the run and after a slew of horrific reviews, the show closed. The recast actors were very quickly and unceremoniously out of work, too.

It happens all the time in the performing arts, which is why actors routinely take "survival jobs" waiting tables while waiting for their next big break. It requires a special mindset, and I was beginning to realize I didn't have it. I couldn't spend the rest of my life being underemployed and constantly looking for work.

I went on to do other national tours and by theatre standards was paid very well, but somewhere between Birmingham and Boston, I knew this was not what I wanted to be doing much longer. I had experienced relative success, climbed pretty high up the ladder, and realized I had placed it against the wrong wall.

Every day, we're climbing ladders. Either professionally or personally, we are all moving up, down, or occasionally taking a breather and standing still.

But what would happen if, like I did, you were making the climb, reached the top (or a plateau), looked around, and came to the conclusion that you were in the wrong place? At the time, I thought I was the only one who spent years leaning against the wrong wall, but it happens to many of us every day.

When we get out of college, we base our hopes and dreams on securing positions at organizations in which we can rise and grow. We get on the ladder and climb away to increase earnings (and maybe power) on the way to the top. However, here's the catch: Once we have arrived at the summit, we may find that it doesn't always make us happy or make us feel accomplished. This may explain why the media barrages us with stories about so-called successful individuals who become involved with drugs, abusive behavior, and, occasionally, suicide. So much effort went into climbing the ladder that they never focused on whether it was the right one.

Oftentimes it starts with parental expectations. Spending my daughter's formative years in New York City I was not only a witness to, but sadly a participant in, the parental pressure to see our kids become superstars. I saw potential notoriety in every one of Avery's activities: child piano prodigy—clearly the next Van Cliburn, winner of a kiddie poetry contest—the obvious successor to Emily Dickinson, figure skating medalist—undoubtedly another Michelle Kwan, and it went on and on, perpetuating through high school and her outstanding college boards. Accepted at almost every school to which she applied, my brilliant daughter (in more ways than one, which you will read about in a minute) narrowed it down to Brown University and Syracuse University.

Here's the catch. My daughter knows the ladder she is climbing. Since age four, despite my misgivings (you'll remember I rejected a career in the theatre), she has had a laser focus and dedicated commitment to performing on Broadway. An acknowledged "brainiac," she chose Syracuse over Brown because SU provided a true music theatre curriculum and Brown did not. At best it would have been ad hoc, nothing like the conservatory experience of the larger, "less prestigious" institution. As decision time drew near, Avery called her unofficial mentor, and my dear friend, for advice. Patty's response was swift and unexpected. "Honey," she said to Avery, "if you go to Brown you'll probably be able to buy the best seats in the theatre. If you go to Syracuse, you'll probably be performing for the people who bought the best seats."

Decision made! While I was blurting out "Brown, Brown, Brown" in the background, Avery boldly pressed the "send" button confirming her acceptance into the performing arts program at SU. The deed was done. As she left the room, she glanced back over her shoulder and triumphantly declared, "Mom, you were going for the prestige. I'm going for the program."

Feeling small and shamed, I was faced with the recognition that, had Avery acceded to my wishes, not hers, she might have found professional success in an alternate field. But would she have found happiness and the personal satisfaction of pursuing her true calling? I would have been pushing her toward my evolved end game, which has come to measure success more in terms of a name on the C-Suite door rather than her name on a theatre marquee. Lesson learned!

In his book *The Pathfinder*, author Nicholas Lore, founder of the Rockport Institute states:

> Over 70% of successful professionals surveyed thought they could have done a much better job of making decisions about their lives. They said that they had not known how to go about making choices in a competent way. In another survey, 64% of college seniors questioned said they had serious doubts that they had picked the right major. Many people put more energy, creativity and commitment into deciding which house to buy or where to go on vacation than in deciding what to do with their lives. More often than not, they drift into a career decision that doesn't really fit their talents or live up to their dreams. Others get stuck along the way and spend their lives making unnecessary compromises.[2]

Margie Warrell, best-selling author of *Stop Playing Safe*, said recently on Forbes.com, "The list of people who sometimes worry about being uncovered as an impostor is as impressive as it is long. So common, in fact, that the term 'Impostor Syndrome' was coined to describe it back in the 1980's."[3]

In a recent study published in the *Interdisciplinary Journal of Contemporary Research in Business*, it was found that job stress dramatically effects satisfaction and performance, especially stress that "results from a misfit between individuals and their environment," (wrong wall). It goes on to state that "when a person is confronted with a situation which poses a threat, and perceives that she or he does not have the capability or resources to handle the stressors, the imbalance that results ... is termed as stress."[4] In my case, the stress was created due to the instability of show-business and I knew I didn't have the emotional resources to continue—I had to move my ladder.

Changing careers can be extremely challenging and personally disruptive, but remaining in a bad situation is often much worse. An article in a recent edition of the *Harvard Business Review* quoted several experts and focused on the consequences of "ladder inertia." "I find a lot of people paralyzed by their unhappiness with their current reality," says Leonard Schlesinger, the president of Babson College and coauthor of *Just Start: Take Action, Embrace Uncertainty, Create the Future*.[5] It's often easier to stay put. "Most people stay too long in bad jobs because the corporate world is geared towards keeping us in roles, not matching individuals up with their ideal roles," says Daniel Gulati, a tech entrepreneur and coauthor of *Passion & Purpose: Stories From the Best and Brightest Young Business Leaders.*[6]

Don't default to inertia! A self-inventory will reveal specific signals telling you if it's time to make a move:

- ➲ You constantly say you're going to quit, but you don't.
- ➲ You don't really want to move up to the next level.
- ➲ You're not realizing your potential.

If any of these signals start flashing, take heed and determine if your situation is truly acceptable. It could be that the toll it is taking on you is not worth sticking around.

Here are some do's and don'ts Gulati finds helpful in deciding it's time to move your ladder.

"Do:

- ➲ Ask yourself whether the job can be done, whether you can do it, and if the costs of doing it are too high.
- ➲ Run short experiments to test whether your current situation is unfixable.
- ➲ Have some sense of what you want to do next before you quit.

Don't:

- ➲ Stay if you don't want the job your boss or another superior is doing—you need to have a vision of what will come next.
- ➲ Burn bridges no matter how dissatisfied you are—it could ruin your professional reputation .
- ➲ Make quitting a habit—you'll blemish your resume."[7]

Moving your ladder requires much thought, strategy, and introspection. So at this point, we need to look at ways to aid us in the process. When I decided that I needed to leave the theatre for a more stable situation, I sat down, made a list of my strengths, and tried to match them to careers I thought I would enjoy, and most important, be good at. This was not as easy as it sounds. Performing a personal inventory is difficult, and not always accurate. I did not have the benefit of a major "self-diagnostic" tool called *"Strengths Finder"* to help me at the time.

If you've been working in corporate America for the past 10 years or so, chances are you've come across *"Strengths Finder."* This revolutionary assessment was created by Donald O. Clifton, an American psychologist, known as "the Father of Strengths Psychology and the Grandfather of Positive Psychology" according to the American Psychological Association. He founded Selection Research, Inc. (SRI) and developed the Clifton *Strengths Finder*, the psychological assessment tool. SRI grew, and in 1988, it acquired the Gallup Organization and took on the older company's name. With coauthor Tom Rath, he wrote *Strengths Finder 2.0*, which has sold more than 4 million copies. The goal of *Strengths Finder* is to help individuals have the opportunity to do what they do best every day. Their research discovered that people spend more time trying to fix their shortcomings rather than developing their strengths. Dr. Clifton wrote, "...to avoid your strengths and to focus on your weaknesses isn't a sign of diligent humility. It is almost irresponsible. By contrast the most responsible, the most challenging, and, in the sense of being true to yourself, the most honorable thing to do is face up to the strength potential inherent in your talents and then find ways to realize it."[8]

The basis for the book is relatively straightforward: We all exhibit personal traits the authors call "talent themes," which, when combined, cause us to hone specific skills better and rise to the top in certain areas, while completely flailing around in others. Once identified, the book includes strategies for applying specific strengths along with website support.

I have attended countless meetings with attendees wearing little badges with lists that include traits such as analytical, arranger, deliberative, focus, include, positivity, woo, empathy, futuristic, maximizer, strategic, and so on. That is a sure sign that they've gone through the *Strengths Finder* exercise and are displaying the results of the comprehensive survey they've taken. After seeing this at so many conferences, I decided to take the test myself and I was surprised how accurate the results were.

I wish *Strengths Finder* had been written when I was in school; I could have avoided many unwise ladder climbs. Better late than never, human resources and training organizations in all businesses are coming to realize the importance of identifying and maximizing their employees' strengths in order to have the right people in the right jobs.

My story had a happy ending. I did continue to put my ladder against several less-than-ideal walls (and did well by climbing to the top each time), but it took several tries before I finally found myself leaning against the wall that was perfect for me. Not everyone is so fortunate.

Let's briefly step back. Before you start looking for walls to lean against, it's important to hone your climbing skills and focus your attention on the ladder itself, as opposed to the wall, when you began to climb. When we're just getting going and pondering our life goals and objectives, we experience pressure to have an articulate response to "Where do you see yourself in the next five to 10 years?" Faced with no concrete answer, many of us, without a set course (that is, no pre-determined wall), literally stop moving, let alone climbing. Inertia sets in as indecision mounts. Unclear as to our career goals, we stop to ponder and eventually petrify. Antidote: keep moving. Skills are transferable, and the idea is to become adept at getting a tochold and rising through the ranks. Conversely, if you've identified the wall but can't perfect the climb no matter where your ladder is leaning, you're going to be stuck on the bottom rung.

The idea is that at the beginning, regardless of the wall, you have to know and understand how to climb upward. Objectives aside, if you don't have the foundational skill set, the climb will be a colossal waste of time. So, regardless of career choice, develop the basic skills that will allow you to eventually accomplish your goals. Staying agile and moving up quickly helps you choose sooner not only what you want, but also what you don't want to do. There are those who say that overall purpose should come first, but quite often, depending on circumstances, purpose changes but foundational needs and desires often do not.

Apparently (and thankfully) the apple doesn't fall far from the tree. My daughter, Avery, just graduated (magna cum laude her proud mother must add) from that intensive and competitive music theatre program at Syracuse University I referenced earlier in the chapter; one of the top five such programs in the country. As I mentioned, she aspires to be a performer on Broadway and in fact just booked her own national tour! But, to support herself while going on auditions, she worked three jobs for seven months. Avery maintains people are unemployed by choice and that in fact employers are looking for motivated employees all the time. She simply used her organizational acumen and the interview (audition) skills she learned for her craft and applied them to her job search. Armed with a fairly scant resume, a winning smile, and a fearless attitude, she covered the West Side of Manhattan making in-person calls. She asked to speak to senior people—meeting with managers from health clubs to baby-sitting agencies to restaurants. Within three days she was actually turning down job offers! Fast-forward to when her cousin came to visit her. Out of school for three years, he was in a funk. He sent out more than 100 resumes and only wanted a job that stimulated him. Avery said, "Make the effort. Show up, engage, and interact. Take anything you can get and make the most of it!" She then shared with him that sometimes at the restaurant when it was slow she just circulated among the tables making small talk, created "to-do" lists, or even ran math problems in her head—anything to stay stimulated and engaged. Apparently my progeny is learning how to climb and I'm pretty sure she'll use her attitude to succeed whether theatre turns out be her right ladder or not.

To be clear, many have succeeded and not dealt with their inner demons, but as a result, they most likely didn't set a particularly high bar to begin with.

Narrowing your scope to be great happens after you acquire the skill to work. Before that happens, you should focus on just accomplishing something! That will give you confidence as well as partially fill your tool box of skills. This primary success will bring you to where you can begin to judge the walls against which you'll lean your ladder and be better able to climb.

In my case, I went through several climbs before I found the right wall—from performing, to TV journalism, to fashion, to public relations, and finally communications. They are all inter-related, they required different skill sets, and without *Strengths Finder*, I had to figure it out as I went along. But here's the thing: I wasn't afraid, even as a parent and breadwinner, to put my ladder against a different wall in order to find the right "climb."

How many of us get stuck, even in elevated positions, unhappy and unfulfilled because we feel our responsibilities are preventing us from moving the ladder elsewhere? How many others are paralyzed because the money we are earning has become a "golden yoke" harnessing us to a life we really don't want?

Strategist Stephanie Holland was one of those initially misguided climbers. She writes:

"Freshly pressed out of university, my peers were seduced by the corporate milk round. By that point we were already chasing an idea of success defined by *the establishment*, which included:

⇨   A massive pay check

⇨   The material possessions it could buy

⇨   The lifestyle that it could afford

Freshly squeezed into the back office at Goldman Sachs, I soon realized the high-flying graduate pay check would never be enough to compensate me for what was required: a zillion hours of work, three PC screens, rude traders, and a bottle of wine a day to cope. I saved for three months and did what any self-respecting idealist would do: travel. Already I knew I was against the wrong wall, however, I would find the right one less than two years later after recalibrating my idea of success, and what it means to me."[9]

Holland figured out that to avoid a crisis once you've reached the top of the ladder, you can set the standards for success that extend past money, and ensure that you can live your life the way you want to. Why is this important? Because once you get past the money, these softer standards can dramatically determine the overall quality of life.

You need to determine:

➲   Wants—and what will money alone get for me?

➲   What exactly does success mean?

➲   How can I make a difference?

➲   How can I impact humanity?

At 22, Holland already knew that money would never be enough, but at the time, there were no role models she could relate to. That's all changed now.

For many, success comes from not only climbing the right wall, but from actually building the wall from the beginning, creating a model for life and success on very specific terms. Blake Mycoskie, author and founder of the iconic shoe company Toms, stated:

People are hungry for success—that's nothing new. What's changed is the definition of that success. Increasingly, the quest for success is not the same as the quest for status and money. The definition has broadened to include contributing something to the world and living and working on one's own terms.[10]

Blake is part of a new group of entrepreneurs that have proven that setting your own standards and terms by defining success in your own way can really be a force for social good as well as material wealth. Companies like Toms (every time someone purchases a pair of shoes, an additional pair is shipped to a youngster in a Third World or developing country), Sseko Designs (making sandals is a vehicle for talented Ugandan women to make money to go to college), Revolution Apparel (who created a one-size-fits-most garment that can be worn more than 20 ways to combat the incredible waste fostered by the fashion industry), Escape the City (an organization dedicated to helping talented individuals find jobs at smaller, entrepreneurial companies as opposed to big companies), and We'ar Yoga Clothing (an apparel collection manufactured with yoga principles at its heart) all involve people who built their own walls to ensure they were climbing to the right place. In my case, the process took a while, but eventually I realized that I had to be in my own business, using my strengths on my own terms to actualize and evolve others. I finally came to the conclusion that in addition to being a strategist, I was a coach and teacher at heart. That's a long way from the stage, but I use my theatre training every day to advise and motivate people to reach their potential. It has turned out to be a perfect wall for me and the climb has been (so far) amazing.

I would be remiss if I did not discuss, albeit at a high level, the fact that there are those who have the right ladder against the right wall, but are going through a period of personal upheaval that may be misinterpreted as job dissatisfaction. A long-standing client of mine, whom I have advised as he's climbed up his ladder, eventually became head of a major consumer healthcare company. He soon decided, however, that the field was not "cutting-edge cool" enough for him, so he jumped ship to head an international fashion house, which I, and apparently many analysts and members of the press, felt was a rather odd choice. At any rate, his tenure at his new job was rocky, almost from the start. He jettisoned established lines, made poor external partner choices, had less-than-positive relationships with the investor and financial community, and eventually drove the company and the stock price into the ground. In four years he destroyed what took him more than 25 years to build. In retrospect, he finally admitted that he should have worked harder at being innovative at his healthcare company, which would have made him feel more contemporary and less "stuck." He moved his ladder from the right wall to a completely inappropriate wall, which became his undoing and the company's. The motto here is look in, look out. Be honest; analyze what's really the source of your dissatisfaction before going to the trouble of moving the ladder you've worked so hard to climb. His story did have an undeserved happy ending: He salved his damaged ego and reputation with a $20 million exit package. Go figure!

Your metrics for success are unique to you. Don't be judged by someone else's idea of it (my family thought I was crazy to leave a senior position and a "safe" corporate job to try to create my own company). Personalize what you want to get out of life professionally and personally and how what you do will affect others. How we elevate and enhance those around us will have defined much of our feelings of success.

First, determine what may be holding you back on the ladder you've chosen, or why you can't change ladders. Maybe you are no longer motivated, work has become tedious, or it is no longer fun. Once you have figured out these negative barriers, it will be easier to jettison them from your life.

Second, go back to the beginning. Determine what got you started on the ladder you chose. I call this defining the "why." If you've read my previous book, *Be The Brand*, you know that I stress the importance of "the why before the what." If you determine why you started on the ladder in the first place, it may be possible to rekindle the passion that will help you re-climb.

Third, prioritize! What's most important to you? If you're frustrated with your current situation, chances are it doesn't allow you to do the things that you really want to do (that is, pursue hobbies, travel, join clubs, volunteer, and so on). Make a list in the order of things that you want to do that will make you the happiest. If what you're doing now doesn't allow that, then it may be time for a change. At the very least, you can determine if you can make adjustments that will allow you greater flexibility to pursue your passions.

Fourth, as you look at your day-to-day responsibilities are you doing what you should? Is your role at work what it needs to be, or have you force-fit yourself into a series of functions in order to have a job? This may work for a short time, but after a while a "square peg in a round hole" will get very sore. If you need to get some additional training, so be it. Cultivate relationships with the right people to help ensure that you are able to have access to the work streams you feel will make you "whole" at work.

Fifth, set boundaries. This is critical. At some point, you have to draw a line in the sand and really understand what you are willing to do and what you will not or cannot do, and you must be able to clearly articulate this (to yourself and to those with whom you work). Flexibility on the job is very important. Even more important is your ability to perform your job at a high standard. And if the demands on you prevent you from doing your best, then everybody loses. Make sure you articulate these boundaries in such a way that it's understood that everybody wins when they are respected.

Finally, let it go! Do a self-check. Remember that perfect is the enemy of good. Maybe you're taking on more work and more responsibility than you should because you're never satisfied with your deliverables or others. At some point, it truly is good enough. As one of my favorite clients, who is promoting a new era of growth for her Fortune 500 Company, declared: "Strive for excellence, not perfection."

When you finally determine how you truly want to live your life and make that climb, the experience will be so much easier. Work becomes pleasure and your passion. But let me be clear: This is not a simple task. It wasn't easy for me, and it isn't easy for most people.

There are many successful people who have climbed ladders to great heights only to find that they needed to move them to a different wall. Both Ron Paul and his son, Rand Paul, began their careers as physicians, but felt the lure of public service and effecting economic policy were more their passions. Giving up a medical career to go into politics was, I'm sure, a difficult decision, but so far, it seems to have worked out well for them both. Chef Julia Child, famously dramatized in the film *Julie and Julia,* was an intelligence officer with the CIA before she realized that her passion was not spying, but cooking. Comic actor Ken Jeong (*Community, Knocked Up, The Hangover*) began his career as a doctor. Elvis Costello was a much-sought-after computer programmer before he turned his sights to music. Andrea Bocelli, world-famous operatic vocalist, practiced law until he was 34, which did not make him happy. He declared that his embrace of singing full-time and leaving the security of being an attorney was the best decision he ever made. As an example that it's never too late to move your ladder, Anna Mary Robertson sold potato chips most of her life and then, at age 80, took up painting. She became known as one of the great American artists, Grandma Moses.

The most difficult piece of this process is being able to walk away when we realize we're leaning against the wrong wall and not feel like we've somehow failed. A good friend and colleague of mine was working in a high-powered law firm in New York for many years. I knew he wasn't thrilled with his job, but was earning a decent living and supporting his family accordingly. One day, I overheard him in a heated discussion with the head of his firm's HR department, and I knew things were becoming rocky. Part of his job included working with individuals in the firm's branch offices, one of which was in Paris, France. On a particular week-long trip to that office, he called me and said, "Can you imagine? I'm having a lousy time in Paris." Right after that trip, he came home and told his wife that he was leaving the firm. He had had enough. He went to his boss the next day and resigned. It was rocky for a few months, but as if a huge weight was lifted from his shoulders, his next climb was almost effortless by comparison. He did find the right wall and has never regretted leaving his big-shot job. That took courage and the ability to handle risk.

Finally, as we close out our conversation around ladders and walls, I would be remiss if I didn't red-flag the following thought.

Sometimes in the paradigm of ladder versus wall, it's not a case of right ladder wrong exterior wall. Maybe it's an "interior" issue, more like a twisted helix versus an ascending stairwell. Could you be holding you back from feeling recognized and ultimately getting rewarded and promoted? According to Wharton School Professor Sigal Barsade, whether or not you are satisfied with your job often has to do with your disposition. Before you declare your job a bad fit, even if you are able to find another one, be sure the problem isn't you, or you will repeat the same pattern and experience the same problems, frustration, and disappointments over again.[11]

"Job searching and changing jobs is not a trivial matter," maintains Gretchen Spreitzer, professor of management and organization at the University of Michigan. "It is often costly to career momentum and earnings."[12] Translation: Sometimes it's better to look *in* than *out*.

I agree with blogger Amber Weinberg, who wisely writes: "I've begun to notice there are three types of people (professionals): the complainers, the doers and the ones that succeed. These three types of people approach their work in completely different ways, and almost always have completely different results."[13]

Amy Gallo, a contributing editor at *Harvard Business Review*, published the following case study that drives home Ms. Weinberg's assertion.

Case Study: Integrate Your Interests Into the Job

The study focused on an engineer in the Johns Hopkins University Applied Physics Lab who found that doing technical work all day was isolating. He took on a new role as a project manager, but was still bogged down with administrative tasks that prevented the interaction with colleagues he felt he needed. Because he wasn't in a position to go out and get a new job, he got some additional training and was able to offer internal presentations and training on tech innovation and creativity. Although these were outside the scope of his role as project manager, he derived much job satisfaction from it and was able to delegate some of his administrative tasks to others eager to perform them. He reported that on a scale of 1 to 10, his job satisfaction went from 3 to about 7, and expected it to go up to 8 or 9 as he continued to incorporate spending more time with people and teaching others.

Briefly put, Gallo says before you move your ladder, "look at yourself, find meaning, alter what you do (shift responsibilities—if not jobs), change who you interact with, resist complaining and keep your options open by expanding your exposure."[14] In other words, focus on developing skills rather than serving time. Figure out what you can learn or join that you can put on your resume. For example, improved computer skills, mentoring new hires, or becoming a part of trade/professional associations.

Frankly, no one said climbing the ladder was easy, but it's much simpler when it's leaning against the right wall—external (or internal)—and you can continue to ascend through the clouds with a brighter sky and clearer horizon.

? Test Yourself!

1.	Why are many people we deem to be successful so unhappy?
2.	What are the influences that shape our initial career decisions?
3.	How does job stress affect performance?

Test Yourself! (continued)

4.	What are the three signals that tell you it may be time to consider moving your ladder?
5.	How can identifying one's strengths help with choosing the right wall?
6.	What is a "golden yoke"? How can it hold you back?
7.	What are the six points that can help you identify the right wall?
8.	Name four successful famous individuals who have had major career changes.
9.	Is the ladder against the wrong interior wall (stairway versus helix)?

Chapter 12

The Essence of *I.C.E.D.*

You will get all you want in life if you help enough other people get what they want.

—Zig Ziglar[1]

Mission Statement
Getting people to act on what you say requires a sequenced strategy.

Anyone who has attended one of our workshops knows that, in addition to alliteration, I love to use easy-to-remember sequences based on common words. Our ability to retain information for any length of time is so minimal that any tool I can come up with to get concepts to "stick" is critical.

A few years ago, in the middle of a seminar, I realized that I needed to take a page from my own playbook and create a memorable frame for the overview portion of the workshop. So much valuable information was being disseminated in a relatively short time, and I knew that, like sand running through an hourglass, most of it would slip away if I didn't present it with a device that could provide immediate recall. After much thought as well as trial and error, "The Essence of *I.C.E.D.*" (Impress, Connect, Engage, Declare) was born. *I.C.E.D.* is a four-step sequence that maps your impact during any communication experience, empowering you to go beyond informing to persuading and getting people to see and hear you—encouraging them to think, believe, and/or act differently.

Why would I devote an entire chapter to this? Because your ultimate success plan, regardless of field or endeavor, will not work unless you can get people to do what you want them to do via visual and verbal acuity. Dr. Albert Mehrabian, professor emeritus at UCLA, laid the foundation for effective communication theory with his two landmark studies published in 1967 and included in a 1971 work titled *Silent Messages*. Through these studies he distilled overall impact into three buckets: content (what you say), non-verbal (how you look), and verbal (how you sound).[2] Content is pretty straightforward: It's the words we use. The non-verbal is more layered—not only how we look facially, but also our personal packaging, attention to detail, animation, and body language. Verbal is vocal production, including volume, rate, pitch, tonal variation, and key stressed words (the clinical name is Paralanguage Elements). Altogether, they total 100 percent of impact in any communication experience, and here's how it breaks down:

Non-Verbal:	55 percent
Verbal:	38 percent
Content:	7 percent

Surprised? How you look and how you sound make up 93 percent of overall impact, with only 7 percent left over for content. When I first read the study, I was shocked. But the more I thought about it, the more it made sense. We see you before we hear you (and what we see colors what we hear), something pop-culture maven Malcolm Gladwell calls "rapid cognition." He describes it in his best-selling book, *Blink*, as "the kind of thinking that happens in a blink of an eye. When you meet someone for the first time...your mind takes about two seconds to jump to a series of conclusions...I think those instant conclusions that we reach are really powerful and really important."[3]

However, as powerful and important as they are, these instant conclusions are not always accurate. Time and time again, we have people making snap judgments about us that are simply not true. Mr. Gladwell tells an interesting story about what prompted him to write the book. Shortly after *The Tipping Point* made the *New York Times* Best-Seller List, the author decided to change his look, letting his hair grow long (and wild). Almost immediately significant changes began to occur. He started getting speeding tickets, was pulled out of airport security lines for extra screening, and ultimately was mistaken for a rape suspect by members of the NYPD. When Gladwell protested, they pulled out a sketch and a description, neither of which matched his appearance at all, except for his hair. After 20 minutes of arguing and persuading, they finally let him go, but that first impression was hard for them to give up. "That episode on the street got me thinking of the weird power of first impressions," said Gladwell.

Sometimes, we don't care what other people think and go about our business driving initial perceptions that are basically irrelevant to us ("Who cares? I'll never see those people again...."). But that's not what your ultimate success plan is about. When putting together your personal success POA (plan of action), what others instantly perceive about you, especially in business, can have a dramatic effect on your ability to be credible, be listened to, and drive action (or, could get you needlessly arrested, as Malcolm Gladwell discovered).

Dr. David Funder is a distinguished professor at the University of California, Riverside, and runs a behavioral psychology laboratory that conducts extensive studies on behaviors that drive perceptions. He noted that two observers can make the same snap judgment about a third person when the judgment is based on specific signals (that is, a limp handshake, ill-placed tattoos, chewed fingertips, excessive cologne, or flashy jewelry). As I discuss during our workshops, people see you before they hear you, and judge you on what they can, which is why, though we like to think we're not superficial, more often than not, we do judge people by their cover.

Oregon State University Professor Dr. Frank Bernieri, who conducts experiments in non-verbal communications, discovered that trained interviewers who conducted 20-minute interviews with job applicants had the same evaluations as those of untrained observers who watched 30 seconds of videotape! He said, "In social psychology, there is what (we) call the 'confirmation bias,' which shows that once we have any expectation, we are biased in the way we process information...first impressions predict final impressions."[4] And these impressions will affect how people interact with you.

I had a real learning experience on a cross-country flight some years ago that has stayed with me ever since. I was upgraded to first class (a consolation prize to those who travel way too much) and was pleased that at least we'd be served some kind of meal. I usually dress for business travel (you never know who's going to be seated next to you), but this time I chose my version of "sweats" (dress jeans and a sweater). At any rate, a rather large gentleman was seated next to me, and, just as the flight attendant was distributing our freshly baked cookies for dessert, I went to the restroom. When I returned to my seat, I immediately noticed that my cookie had disappeared. I turned toward my seatmate and observed many tell-tale crumbs on his jacket. "Did you happen to take my cookie?" I asked. He turned red, hemmed and hawed, and finally admitted that he had. "You were gone for a while, and you didn't look like you wanted it, so I didn't think you would mind." I immediately shot back, "I did, and I do!" I was furious (for some reason, I really wanted that cookie, which made me even angrier at this man's presumption). If I were a well-dressed male, do you think he would have thought that taking the cookie was appropriate? Although, I made an issue out of it with the flight attendant who managed to find me another cookie (while shooting dirty looks at my seatmate), I was still focused on the fact that I had been profiled and deemed unworthy of the cookie (and this man and I had not exchanged one word until I noticed the cookie was gone). I learned then and there that when I travel, I must be more assertive when controlling those initial impressions in order to set appropriate boundaries, and that this could be done within the first 30 seconds of meeting someone. That's when I decided that no matter where I was, my packaging would always be "N plus 1"—in other words, normal for the situation, plus one step up. This has proven to generally give me a leg up and allowed me to take control of those first impressions.

In my previous book, *Be the Brand*, I discussed perceptions in a chapter titled the "Thirty Second Window of Opportunity." A little more generous than Mr. Gladwell, I instructed my readers that it's the first six non-verbal seconds that determine those critical first impressions and if your audience (be it one or many) will deem you worthy (credible), they will stay tuned for what you have to say in the next 24 seconds. If you've nailed that critical half minute, you're more than halfway guaranteed that people will remain with you as you guide them deeper into the sequence of personal brand building we've trademarked as *I.C.E.D.* So let's break it down into its foundational elements.

Impress

In a recent edition of *Forbes* magazine, therapist and leadership guru Carol Kinsey Gorman spoke about the first time you meet a business acquaintance. "The moment that stranger sees you, his or her brain makes a thousand computations: Are you someone to approach? Do you have status and authority? Are you trustworthy, competent, likeable, confident? And these computations are made at lightning speed...in the first seven seconds of meeting."[5] (Gladwell claims two, I claim six, and Ms. Gorman claims seven. The point is judgments are made in less than 10 seconds!)

The whole concept of the importance and immediacy of impressing visually is not new. As a matter of fact, you can trace it back to ancient Egypt. The first female Pharaoh of Egypt, Hatshepsut, adopted the royal dress of her male predecessors in order to impress and underscore her leadership. According to Bio.com, we learn that Hatshepsut depicted herself in "...traditional king's kilt and crown, along with a fake beard and male body. This was not an attempt to trick people into thinking she was male; rather, since there were no words or images to portray a woman with this status, it was a way of asserting her authority."[6]

Throughout history, many other women have taken their cue from Hatshepsut, including Queen Elizabeth I and Joan of Arc. More recently, Hillary Clinton went through several metamorphoses to impress in her roles (from demure First Lady with head bands and fair isle sweaters to hard-working senator in the men's club of the U.S. Senate in dark pant suits to a more colorful compromise as Secretary of State, to a candidate for President). Whatever the role, her packaging has always been strategic with a specific desired outcome in mind. As he transitioned from community organizer to television commentator and presidential advisor, Al Sharpton lost 175 pounds and upgraded his wardrobe to bespoke suits. He is now one of the sharpest-dressed men on television, and his upgraded look and demeanor have directly upgraded his influence. As he pursues higher office, Governor Chris Christie has lost more than 100 pounds and has become a fixture on the Republican circuit around the country. He came to understand the fact that if people couldn't look past his weight, they couldn't hear his message.

Regardless of whether the interaction is professional, social, or familial, the ability to get people to stop and listen with confidence is greatly dependent on your ability to put forth an impressive look and demeanor that are memorable and unique, which are tied directly to you (like any brand, your packaging is critical). Confidence, credibility, and animation all play a huge role in the initial process of impressing and getting/keeping people's attention. Think of the people you know who, when they enter a room, own it. All eyes gravitate to them because of their energy, outreach, and approachability. I recently conducted a keynote in New York City for a group of high-powered women. As each entered the room, the energy became more electric. After about 10 minutes or so, you could see the groups form and the individuals who "held court" with the rest. I found it interesting that even in an assembly of assertive, accomplished individuals, a few rose above the fray and captivated the rest. What did they have in common? Amazing personal packaging with attention to detail, along with facial and vocal animation.

That first six seconds alone may not secure your desired outcome, but it's a crucial element in getting people to stay with you as your interaction progresses.

In addition to impressing visually, you must also impress verbally and virtually. What you have to initially say about yourself is extremely important, and this comes down to your resume when you're job hunting or thinking about changing jobs. The online recruiting site TheLadders.com recently conducted a study on the resume reading habits of headhunters." According to TheLadders.com research, recruiters spend an average of six seconds making a decision on candidates. This particular study focused on an innovative process called "eye tracking." Thirty professional recruiters were enrolled in the study and had their eye movements examined during a specific 10-week period to "record and analyze where and how long someone focuses when digesting a piece of information or completing a task."[7]

The study demonstrated that during the time recruiters spend with resumes (which is really quite short), they check out name, title, company, current position, starting and ending dates, previous titles and companies, previous starting and ending dates, and education.

Because time is clearly constrained, as a potential candidate you need to make it simple for recruiters to be able to glean necessary information by formatting your resume with sequencing and clear layouts. I strongly suggest you avoid distracting visuals (unnecessary photos, logos, and so on), as the study revealed that "such visual elements reduced 'recruiters' analytical capability and hampered decision-making" and kept them from "locating the most relevant information, like skills and experience."[8] An important footnote: There's a general understanding among Fortune 500 recruiters that it's not just what you've done at work; it's what you've done outside of work. What hobbies and skills make you interesting and relatable? We will discuss the all-important interview in a following chapter, but know that you most likely will not get to that level in the process if your resume isn't presented properly.

Your initial virtual communication is also critical. This would be in the form of a "cover letter" for your resume. Your e-mail cover should be short, engaging, and to-the-point: why you are applying, what's in it for them to interview you, and the best way to contact you. I know for a fact that lengthy cover letters, which often restate what's in the resume, are immediate disqualifiers. Nobody has the time, or desire, to read through lengthy e-mail correspondence, so in this case, less is much, much more!

Mark Cenendella, founder and executive chairman of TheLadders.com, has very clear guidelines for e-mail cover letters: "The perfect cover letter is only 2 or 3 paragraphs at most! So please...keep it short and sweet! A great cover letter should make 1 or 2 key points about why you stand out relative to the job or company to which you are applying."[9]

I would go so far as to say this "short and sweet" rule should apply to all of your e-mails; long e-mails are not impressive. They are too labor-intensive (who wants to read them?) and often deleted. Keep your visual communication crisp and engaging, in concert with how you present yourself visually and verbally.

Connect

Once you impress, you must then connect.

In *The Tipping Point*, Malcolm Gladwell talks about the importance of being a "Connector."[10] This is absolutely critical, especially when you are trying to influence without authority—that is, get people to do things (either for you or for a work project) when you don't have any authority over them.

My sister is the Master Connector. She may not be the richest or most glamourous person in the room (although she is quite attractive), but she is most often the most memorable, accruing what Mr. Gladwell calls "social power," and what they call in China (my sister lives in Beijing) Guanxi (connections and relationships). She instantly bonds with almost everyone she meets and gets them to do wonderful things for her. When visiting me recently, she stopped by a local deli. After briefly chatting with the proprietor, he told her, "It doesn't look like I'm going to sell all of these today. Would you like a free dozen bagels?" I have lived in my town for 15 years and have never been offered anything free! Even more amazing (during that same visit) was her junket to the exclusive St. John boutique on Fifth Avenue in New York City. St. John is a very high-end line of women's clothing and my sister waltzed into the showroom carrying a Duane Reade recyclable shopping bag with Lenox Hill Hospital visitors' stickers plastered all over it. She had made daily visits to our sick mother for more than a month and was displaying them like badges of honor. The boutique staff couldn't tell if she was sporting a designer Mochino tote or was in fact a bag lady. But after a few minutes of conversation, my sister had entranced them with her arresting hair (she has a distinctive white streak) and brilliant outreach. She spoke about her "incredible" sibling (me), an author and image consultant, and convinced them to open their showroom, invite me to be a guest speaker for a special evening event (hors d'oeuvres, champagne, and really accomplished women in the audience), and generate some high-end visibility. She bonded with the salesperson helping her, made them interested in meeting me, and said I could hold an audience and convinced them that having an image seminar would be great PR. She didn't even buy many outfits that day. I don't know anyone else who could have pulled it off!

The connect piece is simple, but oh so critical. Whomever you are communicating with must feel that they are getting something out of the conversation (be it live or virtual) within the first 30 seconds. The "something" I am referring to is a benefit. What do I mean by benefit? A benefit is anything that is going to make the other person(s) happier, smarter, or richer. In other words, you have to appeal to their heart, mind, or wallet, and this must happen almost immediately.

The "*30 Second Window of Opportunity*" breaks down as follows: The first six seconds are the "impress" piece, and the next 24 secures the "connect." If the conversation is all about the speaker, and I don't feel there's anything in it for me, I will tune out. We all have attention deficit issues these days, and to keep me engaged, there better be a pot of gold at the end of the rainbow, or I'm not going to stick around.

Time and time again, I've heard professionals—salespeople, marketing people, managers—all think they're being strategic during their "pitch" by mentioning the benefits after a big buildup and reveal. The thing is, by the time we hear what we're getting out of the discussion, we've already moved on. This applies to one-on-one conversations including asking for a raise, asking for a vote, asking for a date—you name it. If you start with the benefits, then the ask is so much easier because we'll want to listen. We are intrigued by "what you can do for me."

Depending on the individual or group, we connect on several levels: viscerally (the touch, mostly the handshake), verbally (Will I like what I'm going to hear?), visually (Is the initial "impress" pulled through?), and virtually (the equity you have built up through previous interactions). As you hone your style, these elements will become automatic. However, initially, you have to pay attention to each in order to guarantee that this connect sequence, supported by the up-front benefits, rolls out appropriately, ensuring that, for the next few minutes, you are being listened to.

An example of an experience when I didn't initially connect proved to be a tremendous learning experience for me. Some years ago I was the keynote speaker at a convention of psychiatrists in Los Angeles. I had spoken to the group the previous year and had gotten great reviews, so they wanted me back. As I prepared for the speech, I thought that it was important that I "upped my game," so I wrote out all my key points on note cards and continually refined them for seven hours on my cross-country flight. I would make a dramatic entrance and wow them with my confidence and authority. I would show those shrinks that I was a real "player." See where this is going? I was making it all about me.

So there I was, waiting to make my grand appearance. The "voice of God" announces me and I enter from the back of the room and stride down the center aisle. "I'm a woman with a mission," I announce profoundly. "My mission is to disabuse you of the notion that the data speaks for itself. A paradigm shift has occurred that requires you to"—as soon as I uttered paradigm shift a hand shot into the air. The attendee stood up and said, "We don't like that. Paradigm shift means HMOs and managed care." Oops! I stopped, swallowed, and said, "Okay, let's call it a new perspective that requires you to engage upfront with attention to detail and personal packaging." As soon as I said that, another attendee stood up and said, "I don't like that. I don't want to be packaged. I don't want to be 'Madison Avenued.' I don't want to be you." (Uh-oh, sinking fast!) I stopped, stepped off the stage, went over to him, and said, "Don't worry: you never will." Everyone else in the room laughed, so I took this as a brief reprieve to "fade and punt." I continued, "Clearly, what I have planned for this morning isn't what you need." I requested a flip chart and then asked them what they wanted to talk about as I scribed a list of subjects for discussion. The funny thing is that the list we ended up with was what I was going to talk about all along. I regrettably served it up in such a way that completely disconnected me from the audience. I learned that if the communication is speaker-focused as opposed to audience-focused, you will never connect. In a nutshell, it's not about you; it's always about them. And if you remember that, you will have a much easier time connecting.

Engage

Engagement is the pull-through of the first two elements: impressing and connecting. This is where the bulk of the communicating occurs, and I have several tips and strategies that will promote engagement.

First, you must frame your comments with inclusive pronouns. Specifically, "I," "me," and "my" must take a back seat to "we," "us," and "our." When you begin comments with "I am here to talk to you about" or "My mission today is to" an invisible wall between you and the individual or group comes crashing down. Engagement is encouraged with "We are here to discuss" or "Our collective mission today is to." I call it "Implied Conversation" and it is a key tool in mastering the *I.C.E.D.* sequence.

In 2008, when Hillary Clinton and Barack Obama were opposing each other for the presidential nomination for the Democratic Party, it became clear, as the campaign unfolded, that Mrs. Clinton was coached to favor "I, me, and my," while Senator Obama used a lot more "we, us, and our." (Remember the Obama campaign slogan "Change We Can Believe In"?) Well, everyone knows how that one turned out. As Obama overtook Clinton, she tried to be more inclusive, but it was too little too late. If you listen to her today, Hilary's tone is much more aligned with her rivals' as she strives to be inclusive and cast a wider net.

Engagement is enhanced through our ability to go beyond mere information transference. Getting into the weeds (micro before you're macro) is something that we're all pretty good at, but does nothing to ensure that the other person is listening and processing what you're saying. It's important to be impactful as you inform, with vocal and verbal resonance. Strategic use of phrases I call, "Focus and Flaggers" emphasize critical information and promote retention. Examples of this include, "Now, if there's one thing to take away from today's conversation, it's..." or "If you're taking notes, you might want to write this down." Judicious use of these triggers will not only promote engagement, but will also help us separate the critical points from the "nice-to-haves." As I mentioned in *Be the Brand*, vocal variation is also a key element here to prevent the "somnambulant drone" that numbs the senses, providing a blank canvas for us to think about something else. You must also continually remind people why what you're saying is important—what we're going to get if we do as you say. If I am benefitting from what you're saying, I will be significantly impacted and, thus, engaged.

It's also crucial that you advance engagement by culling your comments to include only what the group or thought leader needs to hear to get to the desired outcome, as opposed to what you want to say. We tend to give much more information than we need (either to show how smart we are or to give management their "money's worth"), which is unnecessary. Less is more, and when you keep comments brief and focused, you make it much easier for others to be engaged and act on your information.

The aforementioned will not be effective if whomever you are speaking to has disconnected (for whatever reason). It is imperative that you recognize when this happens and facilitate re-engagement. Though I covered this in detail in *Be the Brand*, it's important to mention it again here, as a disconnected listener will not only be disengaged from you, but may take others with him or her. Through physical proximity, benign probing, and animated non-verbal cues, you can go a long way toward facilitating re-engagement, but in order to do this, you must be aware of what's going on with the other person (or group of people) and act accordingly.

Finally, engagement is sealed when everyone feels they have some "skin in the game." There has to be a point when collaboration occurs. If the communication is only one-way, there is a significant risk that there may not be buy-in. Through interactive collaboration, people feel that they have had some say in the outcome and will be more inclined to act accordingly. Again, this is something you must promote as a test of the level of engagement of your audience (be it one or many).

Declare

The final step in this sequence is the one that most people haven't mastered: the art of declaring. What action do you want them to take based on what we've just discussed? You have to be very specific with this and include what's in it for folks if they take the action you are seeking. And when you do this, the words you use are very important. Avoid minimizers like "hopefully" ("Now that we've gone over this, hopefully you'll be able to...”). You don't want to make your call to action optional. Use assertive phrases such as "it's imperative that," "it's critical that," or "it's crucial that we are aligned in order to...." These will drive action, as opposed to "So, now you might want to think about...."

You also want to be specific about the level of commitment you expect—whether you feel they *can* do something, *should* do something, *must* do something, or *will* do something. What is your audience able to tolerate, and what level will drive the action you need and expect?

Declaring is important for another reason. There's nothing more off-putting than to sit through a meeting or conversation and have nothing to show for it. One of the reasons I got out of corporate America was because I couldn't stand the lack of closure at the end of meetings, which always necessitated another meeting! Tell me what you expect me to do and what I get out of it if I do it. That's closure. It will drive action and enhance your brand.

Especially in business, nobody wants to deal with a didactic person who is boring, lacks impact, doesn't connect, and makes it all about them with no benefits to others. Impressing, Connecting, Engaging, and finally Declaring, offers you a simple blueprint to not only promote your success, but also make you a sought-after commodity in your organization. You will empower others to get things done, elevate them as a result, and become someone your colleagues will want to work with. This will speak directly to your leadership skills. Doing something well on your own makes you a good executor. Getting others to do something well makes you a good leader. Let *I.C.E.D.* be the catalyst to enhance your brand by becoming known for an impactful and engaging style that connects and drives action.

? Test Yourself!

1.	What does each letter in *I.C.E.D.* stand for?
2.	What does the Mehrabian study tell us?
3.	In what situations does *I.C.E.D.* come in handy?
4.	What is the significance of the first six seconds?
5.	Describe the importance of hearing benefits early on.
6.	Why are inclusive pronouns important to promote engagement?
7.	Write down two examples of "Focus and Flaggers."
8.	What does successful declaring accomplish?

Chapter 13

Advancing in the 21st Century: "Who and How" in the "New and Now"

Nothing in life is to be feared, it is only to be understood. Now is the time to understand more, so that we may fear less.

—Marie Curie[1]

Mission Statement
When the ladder changes to footholds and the wall looks like a mountain...

My older sister, Rodney (she was supposed to have been a boy), has spent the past 22 years with her husband teaching at international schools, first in Thailand and as I referenced earlier, more recently in China. As an educator and savvy editor I asked her to take a look at *Your Ultimate Success Plan*. She thumbed through the Contents and announced there were two big "misses": "Where are your chapters on cultural differentiation and what about social media? You know they are shaping how we effectively communicate in the new millennium." As a result of living abroad, my sister has developed an unusually keen perspective on dealing with people from different backgrounds and cultures.

Her work requires that she stay constantly abreast of the latest trends in education, and, because she lives on the other side of the globe, her best means is through electronic and social media. While writing this book, Rod informed me that no personal success plan could be complete without considering how small the world has become and how we cannot operate in cultural silos like we did when we were growing up. "How we communicate and to whom we communicate is all different now," she lectured her sister, the communications expert. "You live in the bucolic setting of Princeton, N.J., but even here, via the University, the international presence and its effect on the town is incredible. And with all of the new social and digital media platforms, the need for heightened sensitivities around how and what we relate to people becomes more and more significant." She concluded with, "Homogeneity is *so* 20th century!" She is *so* right!

Whether you're just entering the workforce, a middle manager, or highly placed executive, a keen understanding of ethnocentrism and cultural differences that define so many of us around the world as well as the relatively new channels of communication and outreach available to us, is imperative.

This really hit home during a recent client visit. My company supplies communication strategy services to many business partners. I've been with some of these clients for decades. When I drive to their main office sites and park my car, I feel like family. You know how it is: You're so familiar with the surroundings you don't even look around anymore; you just go about your business. Recently, I had to attend a series of meetings at a particularly tenured client's offices and I had an epiphany of sorts. I arrived early and planted myself outside the conference room in an area near the elevators. With no cell or Internet service, I had the rare opportunity to just sit, look, and listen—and what I noticed surprised me. My "family" had changed. Listening to my "children" walking by me and their animated conversations, it was clear that many of them spoke English as a second language. When I queried someone from human resources later in the day, he informed me that more than 60 percent of the company's associates were from outside the United States, and their countries of origin spanned the globe, including Europe, Asia, Africa, and South America. When did this happen, I wondered? I had been working with the client for many years and all of a sudden I realized how heterogeneous and multinational their workforce had become.

This got me thinking. Each time I went on-site to a different client's office, I tried to find out the same thing: Where did their current employees come from? What I discovered was fascinating. The percentage of foreign-born associates ranged from a low of 35 percent to a high of 65 percent. The rise in nationality-based employee resource groups (e.g. Latin Americans, Asians, and African-Americans) has been tremendous across all industries. In addition, I do not have one client who only does business in the United States. Not only are their partners and customers located internationally, but most of them have offices overseas (or are based in other countries). When I spoke about the trend, no one seemed surprised or phased by it. "That's the way most business are these days" was the general response.

With that realization also came the recognition that doing business cross-culturally (both internally and externally) requires a whole new series of skill sets. Dealing with the many legal and municipal differences is challenging, but more important is the ability to maximize opportunities cross-culturally, sometimes spanning many cultures at the same time within your office group or theirs.

I was informed that from a marketing perspective, targeting specific populations was no longer done through traditional channels (television and print) but through social media (Facebook, Twitter, Pinterest, and so on). Not really new news, but further discussion around the ubiquitous use of these platforms did reinforce the notion that we communicate immediately with a virtually limitless audience whenever we go the digital route. While speed and audience size are an advantage, it also has the potential for permanent and wide-ranging disadvantages. Witness the private e-mails of Sony executives that ended up not being private at all! "Handle with care" needs to be the modern-day mantra, especially when business people use social media for "social" purposes. And although I've discussed face-to-face interactions in great detail, in business, most exchanges are done either via telecoms, video-conferences, WebEx's, webinars, or social media platforms.

A primer on developing your personal success plan would be incomplete without a brief discussion on how, in this century, the rapid changes in the way we interact (via social media and electronic/digital channels) and with whom we interact (regularly, with people from around the world) require strategic thought. Whether dealing with your peers at a meeting, "managing up" with your boss, or dealing with external partners, no one can assume that whomever you are dealing with has a similar perspective to yours.

Live, via phone, WebEx, or social media, today's business associates must be flexible at handling and motivating individuals who come from a wide variety of cultures. The ability to listen is a key attribute, and being able to determine the variety of voices in order to understand what people are really saying is crucial. A cultural blunder could easily undermine an important conversation, relationship, or partnership, sinking the meeting and derailing the deal.

A very good friend of mine, Carol, rose through a series of successful positions in the biotech industry and eventually ran the U.S. division of a multi-national company based in Japan. The Japanese ownership was extremely hands-on and had a distinct way of running things. I advised her that it would be extremely beneficial to develop a deep understanding of the Japanese culture, especially when it came to business dealings. Complicating things was the presence of her U.S. boss, an ambitious, smart executive who brought her in when the company was expanding to basically pick her brain. He was sharply tuned into the Japanese culture and used it to his advantage. Long story short, things got a bit dicey regarding some business practices and Carol tried to do an end-run around her boss with the Japanese who, of course, neither appreciated her perceived lack of loyalty nor really believed her story over her alpha male boss. While completely blameless regarding the questionable practices, my friend was walked out the door following a strategic meeting between her boss and his Japanese superiors. He was a master cross-cultural manipulator while my friend was merely "right." In this case, "right didn't lead to might," and Carol lost big time. Had she had less contempt for her Asian bosses and a more strategic way of handling her own boss, she could have survived the situation. A hard lesson was learned.

Hierarchal relationships vary greatly between cultures, which Carol did not totally embrace. Guido Gianasso, vice president for human capital with the International Air Transport Association, "points out that Chinese, Indian and most other Asian cultures are extremely collectivistic, with relationships governed by high 'power distance'—a sharp awareness of differences in status."[2] He continues, "However, most international companies have their roots in the western European/North American cultures, which tend to be more individualistic with lower 'power distance.'" Although as Westerners we tend to be more egalitarian in our approach, we must continually recognize that many cultures aren't (thus our continued difficulties dealing with such countries as Iraq, Iran, and Pakistan). This is also exacerbated by what many of us exhibit as cultural arrogance and a feeling of superiority ("You're in our country now and we always know best!"). In addition, change is difficult for most people and the shock that sets in when we must make a transition through new cultural awareness ("What do you mean we have to have dinner first before we discuss business?").

We are famous (or infamous) for our insatiable thirst for market research. The data we yield from such initiatives has become a panacea for marketing decision-makers ("Well, the survey said this, so it must be so!"). I, therefore, find it incredible (and occasionally funny) that well-intentioned, seemingly well-informed companies make huge blunders when it comes to cross-cultural endeavors. The following are a few examples.

- ➲ A contrite group of U.S. executives was chagrined when they realized that the name of a vegetable oil being marketed in Latin America, when translated from English into Spanish, was "Jackass Oil."

- ➲ A prominent U.S. auto manufacturer tried to sell its new muscle car, the Matador, with images of courage and strength. The problem was that in Puerto Rico, "Matador" is equated to being a killer, and so it was no wonder that potential buyers were deterred from using it on the notoriously difficult roads on the island.

- A telephone utility in the United States launched an advertising campaign targeting the Latino market with a commercial featuring a Latino woman demanding that her husband call their friends explaining that they will be late for a dinner engagement. The ad was a flop because Latino women generally do not make such demands of their husbands, and a call about being late for dinner would not be made.

- A fragrance company used the same picture (a warm-hearted scene with a dog and his master) for Western countries as well as Islamic countries. It did not do well in the Islamic world, as dogs are felt to be unclean there.

- A huge consumer products company broadcast a commercial in several Asian counties, including Japan, which proved to sell well in Europe. It featured a woman in a bath with a man (presumably her husband) coming into the bathroom and caressing her. Unfortunately, in Japan, this was felt to be in very bad taste, as the Japanese feel that such an action would be considered a privacy invasion and inappropriate.

- While in Saudi Arabia, an American businessman turned down the hospitality of a cup of coffee from a Saudi-Arabian colleague. This was considered incredibly rude and effectively halted all business negotiations thereafter.

My own example:

- During a performance evaluation, a Japanese executive with an American company was required to give critical feedback to an employee. Traditionally, Japanese find it rude to deliver direct, to-the-point criticism, and this was causing a severe comprehension problem. I was asked to help him with his "leadership style." I explained that he was working within his cultural norms and then explained to him that he had to adapt and work within ours, or at least move closer. The executive took many attempts before he could muster enough directness to talk about the sub-par performance to his American subordinate and be clearly understood.

What do all these anecdotes have in common? A little bit of human research and sensitivity would have gone a long way toward eliminating the negative fallout from each of these incidents. The lesson is: your way is not their way. How you interpret things may not be their way of perceiving things. When working across cultures (and genders, by the way), you can never forget this. Our trademarked *Role of Receivership* really applies in these instances!

The concept of "Power Distance" (PD) comes into play, especially in a multicultural business environment.

What PD measures is the particular equality/inequality between members of a society. Any nation with a high PD score not only accepts, but also maintains the inequalities that are perceived between members of the society. The caste system in India is a perfect example of what would constitute a country's high PD score. Conversely, a lower score on the PD scale would indicate that the society is not focused on differences between its members' wealth or power. A more egalitarian attitude is common as is upward mobility.

Guido Gianasso observed that it is common for junior members of a team "...from low-power-distance cultures...U.S. or U.K., to throw out ideas and volunteer" for assignments. By comparison, "junior Chinese... were extremely cautious...before daring to intervene" until senior team members had presented their ideas first.[3] Rather than impose a particular culture on a group, in order to nurture a successful multicultural organization, it's better to be a cross-cultural bridge spanner, usually championed by bicultural employees who have lived in several cultures and are more sensitive to cross-cultural environments. Seek them out and bring them in. Everyone needs a modern-day Sacagawea (the famous scout and interpreter for the Lewis and Clarke expedition).

Geert Hofstede, a Dutch social psychologist, is well known for his pioneering research of cross-cultural groups and organizations. He devised the four dimensions of cultural theory that help us identify and deal (or not deal) with inter-cultural differences.[4] In addition to *Power Distance*, they also include *Individualism* (the degree to which a culture reinforces the rights of individuals versus a more collectivist culture; does everyone's opinion need to be considered or can we drive action with consensus?), *Uncertainty Avoidance* (the degree to which a culture tolerates change, ambiguity, and experimentation; how conservative/risk-taking can our actions be?), and *Masculinity* (how specific groups emphasize [or don't emphasize] the established masculine stereotypes regarding work, achievement, power; are women and men regarded more or less as peers?). Examination of how specific cultures actualize these dimensions not only elevates cultural awareness, it can also help maximize the contributions of individual members regardless of where they come from, with your recognition and encouragement.

As I mentioned earlier, cultural differences are gender-based as well. Issues between men and women are as old as time. For example, the number of women in the workplace is beginning to exceed the number of men. In terms of compensation, power, and ownership, however, the business world (and the professions) are still male dominated. Although I have no intention of getting into a lengthy discussion on the need for parity between men and women to drive better outcomes, certainly there needs to be sensitivity around the differences between the genders and how we can get the most from people within a culture's context toward the roles of men and women.

Every society has varying attitudes toward how men and women should/ do function. Although men and women can often perform the same duties (from a technical standpoint) each gender responds differently to specific situations as they carry out their responsibilities. Our tolerance and embrace of these differences goes a long way toward maximizing someone's performance. If you think about it, the level of reactions experienced by people exposed to a variety of cultures can be compared similarly to the levels of reactions toward gender behaviors of the opposite sex. Cross-culture awareness must include cross-gender awareness. Patricia Heim, PhD, author of the best-seller, *Hardball for Women*, cites the following when describing male and female workplace behavior: "For men, wielding power is natural, desirable and masculine...whereas for women, it's important to keep power dead even." She maintains that the different genders approach success from different ends of the spectrum. Translation: Cross-culture awareness must include cross-gender awareness![5]

According to a seminal Catalyst Study, gender stereotyping still exists. The majority of very senior U.S. business managers still find women leaders in their organizations exhibiting "caretaker" behaviors, such as supporting others and rewarding subordinates.[6] Conversely, they perceive male leaders to be more effective at "take-charge" behaviors, such as delegating and problem-solving. In a separate study entitled "Different Cultures, Similar Perceptions" the Catalyst think tank maintains the *same* stereotyping exists in major countries around the world, citing Anglo-Germanic, Latin, and Nordic cultures holding the *same* views.[7] Your mission: Be aware and try to repair. Although stereotyping is time efficient (that whole snap judgment phenomenon), in the end it makes you look small and very often wrong. Climbing your success ladder starts with bending the curve!

One of the major facilitators of cross-cultural awareness, especially among countries, has been the evolution of the slavish use of social media. What was originally intended as a tool for bringing people together for *social* purposes has turned into a huge engine that contains more and more *business* content.

Rebecca Sawyer, from the University of Rhode Island's honors program in communications, notes that, "New social media have become increasingly popular components of our everyday lives in today's globalizing society. They provide a context where people across the world can communicate, exchange messages, share knowledge, and interact with each other regardless of the distance that separates them."[8]

For your personal success plan (to truly be successful) it's critical to understand that social media is becoming a major element of most business's marketing outreach—targeting specific audiences and populations. It is no longer perceived as a "platform du jour."

Where you could once attract and promote with a traditional website, think future—replaced and eclipsed by mastering the tools social media offers. For example, the interactive nature of Twitter allows companies to engage in robust discussions directly with a targeted customer base, which is much more powerful than traditional direct-to-consumer advertising.

Knowledge is the stepping-stone to success, so as you make your upward climb, keep these statistics in mind, courtesy of a recent edition of the Social Media Marketing Industry Report: (a) almost every business that has a marketing department uses social media as an integral element of their marketing plan; b) half of the critical demographic, people ages 20 to 29 spend at least 10 or more hours per week perusing social media sites; c) 90 percent of those businesses who use social media as part of their marketing plan experienced an increase in their marketing reach; and d) 65 percent of businesses that have used social media as part of their marketing strategy for a three-year-period have reported greater earnings for that period of time.[9]

If you want to be recognized, rewarded, and promoted, being a social media maven is a sure way to do it. In order to assume this mantle and build an effective social media marketing platform, you must understand the basic as well as subtle characteristics of your organization. For example, consider the size of the company. A bigger organization is going to have attributes and needs that will demand a totally different social media plan than a smaller one. Focus on what will work for your particular business. A bigger company will need to reach out to a larger target to get national recognition for their products and services. A smaller, local-based business can use social media to establish a customer base with a more personal approach. A product or service that is aimed at individual customers can be sold via social media as contemporary and "hip." Basically, your company, regardless of size, can leverage its points of differentiation with a social media platform.

One of my long-term clients is a pioneer in the use of digital marketing/social media to engage with specific niche customer populations—people whom they would never have been able to reach with traditional channels. Their programs have won awards and have directly increased their market share. However, it took a while to get the initiative going because of the various internal regulatory and compliance hurdles it had to pass before going live.

A few things to be aware of:

- ⮑ Social media enables the spread of unreliable or false information.

- ⮑ Social media sites do not have controls in place to prevent intrusions (private, corporate, government, or otherwise).

- ⮑ Use of social media can potentially harm job prospects (most job recruiters thoroughly search the internet/social media sites) when determining qualifications for job candidates).

- ⮑ Social networking sites' advertising policies often constitute an evasion of privacy (don't you love those pop-ups?).

- ⮑ Social media posts cannot be completely deleted and can have unexpected/unintended consequences.

- ⮑ Social networking sites are vulnerable to security attacks including identity theft.

Despite the issues listed, social networking is here to stay, and right now the pros exceed the cons for most of us. And in business, if you haven't already jumped on the Facebook/Twitter/Pinterest/Google/Instagram bandwagon, you will. So, a word of caution: If you want to post something personally, the criteria I use is that if it's not fit or appropriate for your mother to read, don't post it! In business, if you don't have a group that oversees social media, then ask a colleague before you post. If you're a solo practitioner, consult a marketing or PR professional. Never forget that once something is sent out digitally, no matter what "they" tell you, it's out there forever and cannot be recalled.

In truth, regardless of the medium, it's very difficult to recall things that we say. This chapter would not be complete without some awareness and tips around other forms of virtual communication (telecoms, Skype, webinars/WebEx, video conferences). More and more, face-to-face exchanges are being deemed too inefficient, too time-consuming, and too expensive. Meetings, conversations, and presentations are being conducted through virtual channels. Telephone conferences, video conferences, webinars,

Skype, and WebExes have become central to our professional and personal communications. We prize them for their economy (much cheaper than live interactions), efficiency (unlimited participation, facility-free), and ease (advanced hardware and software are user friendly and effective). What we don't do is measure their actual productivity. Studies have overwhelmingly demonstrated that quality retention and execution of next steps dramatically decline when comparing virtual to live communications. But virtual is here to stay, and probably increase, so attention must be paid. And there are specific strategies that will allow you to maximize output and meeting results even when conducted over the telephone, web, or cyberspace.

Whenever I plan a meeting or presentation, live or virtual, the questions I always ask myself are "What do they have to leave with that they didn't have coming in" and "Why should they care?" When I answer that question, I am able to come up with a simple agenda. With studies demonstrating that we retain less than 10 percent of what we hear, I find it puzzling that managers are still conducting extensive telecoms or webinars with complex agendas and actually expecting participants to remember and take action on every point discussed. I know several top companies that conduct annual sales meetings over the web lasting six hours! Less expensive? Yes! Productive? I don't think so.

Whether you're conducting a telecom or webinar, know that after about 45 minutes, there's a significant drop in attention, retention, and participation. I strongly suggest that no virtual meeting go on for more than an hour. An over-ambitious agenda does not make the meeting more productive; it merely creates more potential points of failure to generate pull-through.

Sometimes a longer meeting can't be avoided, so here's a tip. Whether it's an hour or more, it's imperative that every 10 minutes or so, you insert what I call an internal summary. This will allow you to "chapter" the previous chunk of the meeting and bring people who have disconnected up to speed. It also allows you to repeat key points, which drives greater retention. It goes something like this: "So we've covered A, B, and C, which leads us to D." If you're conducting the meeting over the web with slides,

I suggest you insert blank or logo slides with no real content during these summaries, so the focus is on the narration without the distraction of a visual. These internal summaries will go a long way to making sure the meeting's desired outcomes are met.

Facilitate, Facilitate, Facilitate...

When conducting a telephone conference, there are certain rules of the road that will help drive retention as well as action and desired outcomes.

1. Make sure that you announce to everyone who is on the line (and live with you), so we know who is participating.

2. Announce to everyone on the phone what the overall goal of the telecom is so people can guide their comments and contributions toward that desired outcome and avoid extraneous input.

3. Do not allow more than one conversation to take place at the same time. Sidebars are extremely disconcerting during telecoms, especially to those who have phoned in and can't hear what's being said.

4. Each time someone speaks, insist that they identify themselves. It's important to know who is saying what and, over the phone, voices are easily confused.

5. Have a hard copy of the telecom attendance list. Every time a participant makes a comment, a tick should be placed next to their name. Eventually, you will have a list with some names having many tick marks and some having little or none. It's a good bet that the ones who have a small number or no marks next to their name have either disengaged or are in disagreement with what's being discussed. Either way, you need to facilitate their involvement. If they're disengaged, they are not going to take action on what needs to be done, and if they disagree with what's being discussed, they can sabotage next steps. The "good, bad, and ugly" must be articulated on the call, when you can control it, as opposed to after the call, when

you can't. So, if you see someone has not been participating, bring them in with a softball question that is easy for them to answer, but doesn't "call them out." A simple question will encourage risk-free participation while a blatant call-out ("Hey John, are you still on the line? Haven't heard from you yet.) will turn off not only John, but everyone else on the call. Chances are they will pay more attention if they know they may be asked direct questions. If they have an issue with what's being discussed, this will also allow them an easy entry into the discussion.

6. As stated earlier, every 10 to 15 minutes, articulate an internal summary that will allow you to repeat key points and bring those who have disengaged up to speed.

7. At the end of the meeting, call out the next steps and who will be responsible for them. Immediately following the call, send out an e-mail with these assigned next steps as a paper trail. Without this kind of pull-through, it's difficult to hold participants accountable.

Whatever the venue or when conducting meetings/presentations over the phone, computer, or iPad, know that certain adjustments are necessary to ensure that participants feel valued and are engaged and understand the next steps in order to achieve desired outcomes. If you plan in advance accordingly, chances are that when you announce the next virtual meeting, your audience won't immediately make plans to multi-task.

Though the use of digital communication and social media has its detractors and issues, we cannot turn back the clock, and its effective use has proven to be a boon to individuals, organizations, businesses, and consumers. It is critical, however, that safeguards be put into place in order to protect the companies for which we work, as well as ourselves as individuals. There once was a time when you could decide whether or not your life was an "open book." With the advent of digital communications and social networking, that window is closing fast.

Needless to say, the cross-cultural issues discussed earlier in this chapter apply to virtual communications as well as face-to-face encounters.

Technology has made the world much smaller, and I strongly feel that we are so much better off because of our increased ability to tap a wider variety of perspectives, viewpoints, and skill sets through cross-cultural collaboration. And through either myopia or our own cultural biases, if we fail to leverage the significant assets that a wide variety of cultures bring to the table, both internally and externally, our success plan will be severely hampered.

In addition to making sure your ladder is placed against the right wall, you need to make sure that you are climbing a well-placed ladder! The vastly multi-cultural "one world" in which we live, in tandem with the lighting-like speed of the evolution of social/digital media, requires us to re-examine our climb at every rung. As my sister noted, homogeneity is so yesterday. Don't be stuck in the 20th century; master the new and the now by understanding the who and the how.

? Test Yourself!

1.	What is meant by "Homogeneity is so yesterday?"
2.	What is the current trend regarding the nationalistic/cultural makeup of the associates at most businesses in the United States?
3.	How does the concept of "Power Distance" affect relations between along various levels of an organization?

Test Yourself! (continued)

4.	How does gender come into play when discussing cultural diversity?
5.	How does the use of social media vary from company to company? What are the considerations?
6.	What are some of the personal/professional dangers around the use of social media?
7.	How can social media be used to market to specific populations?
8.	Do you have any qualities that could be considered as gender bias?
9.	Rate your social media savviness.

Chapter 14

It's Showtime!

There will be time, there will be time
To prepare a face to meet the faces that you meet.

—T.S. Eliot[1]

Mission Statement
Interviews: It's all about the audience.

When I was a young girl, money (like it is for so many of us) was a real issue. I was determined to graduate from high school with honors (which I did), get into a great college (which I did), and pay for most of it myself (which I wasn't sure I could do). While I worked nights and weekends at Lett's Fashions as a sales clerk, the most I could pay for was my wardrobe (which made me the envy of the "in-crowd" and welcome at every cafeteria table in my high school). What it didn't do was provide leftover income for my higher education.

Determined to help my strapped parents, who were already over-extended (sending my sister to an elite private college), I chanced upon an ad in *Seventeen Magazine* that proclaimed, "You too could be the next Miss Teenage America." The thought had never occurred to me, but when I read about the college scholarship that went with the title, I immediately filled out the application form and sent it in with my year-book photo. Several weeks later, I learned I had made the first cut and was being invited to become an "official" contestant. Much hard work, family sacrifice and support, and anxious elimination rounds later, I was crowned Miss Teenage Michigan! I went on to compete at the national level, and though I didn't capture the title, I was a runner-up and winner of the talent competition, which netted me a generous scholarship. Mission accomplished!

What the experience taught me was that attitude and stamina counted as much or more that brains and beauty. The girls who prevailed exuded energy and engagement. For us it was a 10-month audition marathon from the state to the national competition—constantly being judged, constantly on our game, constantly staying positive. Long before Bob Fosse coined the phrase "It's Showtime!" we were living it.[2]

Fast-forward half a lifetime later and that is exactly the way I feel before each workshop I conduct, each time I pitch business to a client, each time I deliver a keynote, and each time I have to conduct an inter-view or be interviewed. Even at this stage in my career, I always have to "audition" for business. It's somewhat like job-hunting, except I often have to convince the potential client that they have an open position that they didn't know they had. ("You don't need my help? Oh, yes you do, and here's why....) Mastering the skill of always being interviewed is a critical part of any personal success plan.

There are books and articles galore on interviewing techniques, how to wow a potential employer, how to land the job, and so on. The fact of the matter is that, although mastering the art of the all-important job interview is critical, the skills you need to sharpen will apply to the many other "interviews" you experience on almost a daily basis. During these interactions, you have to, in a relatively short time, inform and persuade, which is basically the function of an interview, be it formal (applying for a job, loan, or country club membership; buying a co-op apartment; or even your annual review) or informal (cross-functional business planning, chatting up the "big boss" in the company cafeteria, professional develop-ment planning with your HR representative, or trying to get out of a traffic ticket).

However, because the job interview is becoming more and more important (and critical as we tend to hop from job to job more often), we need to focus on that process—albeit from a perspective you probably haven't yet come across.

First, and most important, your skills, credentials, and accomplishments are *not* the critical considerations of those conducting the interviews. Your resume and recommendations got you in the door. If they didn't feel you were qualified for the job, they wouldn't have called you in. What they are looking for is the all-important "fit." Do you fit into the culture of the company? Do you fit into the department in which the job sits? Would people appreciate spending eight hours a day with you?

With face-to-face touch points so rare these days, the interview is the best opportunity for you to establish yourself as a viable candidate and make a good impression. It's all about how you present yourself, deal with questions (and answers), and let the interviewer feel that having you around would be a definite asset to the company as well as the people who work there. Attention to detail is critical. The slightest misstep could derail the entire conversation and will disqualify an otherwise-ideal candidate. The gene pool is just too large and these days interviewers look more for reasons to filter a candidate out as opposed to bringing someone in.

As someone who has spent much of my adult life interviewing potential hires or being interviewed, I can say with authority that a significant portion of anyone's overall impact when vying for a job takes place before you utter a single word. A short anecdote sums it up best: When my niece was looking for a summer job recently at a competitive consulting firm, her recruiter informed the candidates, "I know within the first 10 seconds if I'm going to consider someone for a second interview. The other four minutes, 50 seconds is merely a courtesy."

Tough to hear? Absolutely! But it validated what I have been teaching my clients for more than 20 years (and what you've already read so far): It's about telegraphing who you are before you tell me why it matters. We call it executive presence, and it applies to your facial engagement and personal packaging—that is, the energy you bring into the room, personal introduction, body language, and overall attitude.

We've all heard it time and time again: "I hope they like me," "I hope they like my outfit," "I hope I don't look nervous," "I hope I remember to smile." What's the common word here? *Hope!* Well, hope is not a strategy (the title of a well-known self-help book), but let me add my own mantra: *Success Is a Planned Event!* What this means is that success is not a matter of luck or happenstance. It's the result of devising useful strategies, application, and attention to detail. You may not be guaranteed a second interview in the first 10 seconds, but you can be guaranteed you won't without the proper planning. Here's how to apply much of what we've already discussed to a critically important part of the professional experience: the interview. And you start by working from the outside in!

A recent study conducted by Susan Fiske of Princeton University, Amy Cuddy of Northwestern University, and Peter Glick of Lawrence University titled "Universal Dimension of Social Cognition" discusses that when it comes to first impressions, we base our perceptions on two components: warmth and competence.[3] Are you engaging with the intentions that will benefit the organization, and are you able to perform at a level that will deliver on those intentions? How you communicate these two qualities in any exchange will define your ability to get the gig.

Personal Packaging

What do so many well-intentioned job seekers do prior to an important interview? They buy a new outfit! This seems to be a default plan of action, and unfortunately not a good one. When you wear something for the first time, you're not exactly sure how it's coming off, and you spend a great deal of psychic energy wondering if you look good and feeling self-conscious. It's much more effective (not to mention comfortable) to wear an outfit that you know makes you look good and shows you off, sort of like bringing a best friend with you. As a result, you will enter the room with more confidence because you don't have to think about how you look. In addition, I suggest that once you're dressed for any interview, you take the opportunity to glance at yourself front and back. Don't forget: Your back is the last thing your interviewers will see, and you don't want to leave with anything but a good impression; reinforce the "wow" factor coming and going.

It's important that you do your research and find out what the culture of the company is and what the dress code expectations are. After that, you need to ramp it up at least one level when you come in for an interview (N + 1). Unless you are dressed in overly formal attire (what you'd wear to go to an evening wedding), you will rarely be faulted for being "too dressed up." I am always impressed when candidates take the opportunity to dress well for an interview. I am also always dismissive when a candidate is too informal in their attire without attention to detail.

In addition, I almost always know when someone is "dressing the part" or is feeling natural in the clothing they've chosen to wear. Unless you're in the military, a "uniform" (something you would never wear unless the job required it) is quite unnecessary. The days of the "gray flannel suit" are over and it's important to express some individuality while conforming to the expectations of the organization.

In her best-selling 2011 book, *The Underdog Edge*, author Amy Showalter writes, "It's important to dress *appropriately* for the situation and let your personal style come through. You can do that and still show respect to those you are petitioning. In fact, failure to do so communicates the fact that you care more about yourself and your comfort and your 'style' than the person you want to persuade. Remember, it's about *them* and not *you*."[4]

Pre-Interview Preparation

Preparation is key. An actor would never think of walking on a stage without rehearsal. You need to think of an interview in the same way. The more prepared you are, the more relaxed you'll be, and the more relaxed you are, the more confident you'll come across. It's that simple. (Remember: It's showtime!)

Assuming you've been interviewed before, you pretty much know the questions you're going to be asked. Review them and practice your responses (with a trusted confident or in front of a mirror). Canned responses are generic and forgettable. For example, say you are asked "What do you feel is your major weakness?" and your response is "Well, people have told me that I can be relentless and work too hard." Please.

You need to come prepared with honest responses (interviewers appreciate honesty, by the way) and articulate them in the form of stories that illustrate things like your strengths, flexibility, leadership, desire to take on responsibility and learn new skills, problem-solving/solution driving, and business community involvement. We love stories, and they are so much more memorable than plain responses. Also, a story cannot be challenged or contradicted; it's uniquely yours.

As I mentioned earlier, you wouldn't be called in for the interview if they didn't feel you were qualified for the job. But it doesn't hurt to remind them how your qualifications directly relate to the job requirements. So before the interview make a list of all the listed expectations and correlate each to your skills. This process may uncover a hole in your skill set, which is not necessarily a bad thing. Plan how you will respond to this if it should come up in the interview so you can persuade the recruiter that you are up for learning a new skill.

Though I'm sure you know that you should come into the interview with a list of prepared questions, make sure they go beyond the usual "What is the vacation policy for new hires?" and ensure that they reflect that you've done some research on the organization ("Can you give me an example of how an employee resource group has been able to effect company policy?" or "What does the company's five-year plan look like?").

Facial Engagement

In my previous book, *Be the Brand*, I discussed the importance of "Giving Face." The face is a professional's stock and trade, and it speaks volumes. Animation is essential. Scientists tell us there are 70 muscles in the face capable of thousands of different expressions; make some! In the course of interviews, be memorable, stand out from the masses, and use your face. As simple as it sounds, it bears mention here: A smile is an imperative (not a nervous one, but one that says you're happy to be there). Here's a little-known fact: by smiling you release endorphins, which reduces stress. So you not only look energized, you feel energized as well. You should also make eye contact with everyone in the room (if there's more than one person doing the interviewing). Make sure you include everyone who might be involved in assessing your potential, not only your potential new boss. When you're asked questions, be sure to be strategic, and wait a beat before responding even if you know exactly what you plan to say. This will make you appear thoughtful as opposed to impulsive. It is critical not to interrupt an interviewer and complete his or her sentence, even when you know where the conversation is going. In addition, while non-verbal engagement is essential (smiling, an occasional nod of recognition and/or approval), too much nodding indicates impatience. (For example, "I know where you're going with this, so you can stop speaking and let me respond.") Again, a mirror is a great tool to see how animated you can be when responding to questions.

Energy

Remember: Energy is infectious. If you don't have it, they can't catch it, and the judging begins the second you come into eyesight.

So when you introduce yourself, it must be with animation and confidence, ensuring that the focus is on you. Otherwise, everything you do next will drown in that dreaded "sea of anonymity." (Remember that 30-second window of opportunity discussed in a previous chapter? It goes by very quickly!) When you walk into the room where the interview is taking place, enter with a confident stride and start speaking as you come into eyesight. So many interviewees wait until they get right in front of the interviewer before they begin to speak. Those few precious dead seconds give the interviewer time to pre-judge you or, worse, disengage. An authentic, "Good morning! Thank you for seeing me today!" spoken with volume and authority immediately upon entering the room will get and retain their attention. Again, it's so much easier to find reasons to reject as opposed to reasons to engage. Don't give them the chance.

Visceral Connect—The Handshake

A well-executed handshake is an absolute must! I have personally seen many outstanding, qualified job candidates sent to the reject pile because of a poor handshake. This is a make-it-or-break-it connection that is not difficult, but does require some thought. First, do not wait to extend your hand until you're just a few feet away from your interviewer. When the other person comes into eyesight, say 12 feet away, extend your arm fully (no 90-degree bent elbows). The interviewer will mirror you and do the same thing. What this creates is an additional 3 feet of space between you, allowing an accommodation for height differential and an elongated moment of connection. When you do shake hands, make sure the grip is "web to web" with the space between the thumb and index finger flush against the same space of the interviewer's hand. The grip should be firm, but not crushingly so. You should hold the other person's hand approximately two to three seconds before releasing. A good handshake will set a wining tone. A creepy one will kill it!

Dr. John Sullivan is an internationally known HR thought-leader from the Silicon Valley. In his widely read book, *1,000 Ways To Recruit Top Talent,* he discusses the importance of the handshake:

> [We] know that the handshake and (the candidate's) appearance are the two most powerful elements that contribute to that powerful first impression The fact that assessing handshakes is a major hiring decision factor is not just conjecture; research from Greg Stewart of the University of Iowa demonstrated that those with the best handshake scores were considered to be the most hirable by the interviewers. Handshakes also proved to be more impactful than "dress or physical appearance."
>
> Handshakes become a high-impact problem because handshakes occur in every interview, and a single bad handshake can immediately eliminate a top candidate, especially in entry-level jobs. You should also be aware that handshakes with women candidates leave a bigger impression and have their own unique set of biases. No one has ever been sued over handshake bias but the loss of top candidates as a result of it is real.
>
> Every job candidate should realize the importance of handshakes. However, if you are a candidate who experiences very short interviews or if you are frequently dropped after one initial interview, you should also be aware that how you shake hands may be a primary reason for it. Every candidate should learn about each of the dozen or so handshake errors that they can make (fortunately, a majority of them can be overcome through practice and criticism). In addition, they should learn and practice the characteristics of a

great handshake. Closely watch the eyes, the facial expression, and the body language of the interviewer immediately after a handshake. Because through this observation, you may be able to catch the fact that you made a major "handshake error," so that you can then quickly work to overcome it.[5]

I've been talking about the importance of the handshake for more than 20 years, and it's amazing how many incredibly qualified job applicants are thrown on the reject pile because of a poor handshake. Spend the time to perfect this simple connection tool so you can begin the conversation by putting your "best hand" forward!

The following story illustrates the point. Several years ago, as a communications and image consultant, I was asked by a huge consumer company to screen potential new hire candidates. One in particular rose among the rest. On paper he was exceptional—great credentials including a newly minted MBA from Harvard. I was convinced this Ivy Leaguer was a shoo-in. In fact, I didn't see the need for an interview but felt we should conduct one as a formality. The candidate met separately with his potential boss, the head of HR, and me. When we assembled later for our debrief, none of us even got to his qualifications; all we could comment on was his "creepy handshake." Mr. Right instantly became Mr. Wrong and we wrote him a rejection letter the same day. Poor guy, I'm sure he never knew why he was turned down and I've felt a little guilty all these years that I didn't provide him with honest feedback.

Be Prepared to Take Notes

This applies to meetings and any sort of interview, be it informal or formal: Bring a pad and pen to take notes. Even if you have absolutely no interest in taking down anything that is said during the interview, the act of writing down significant responses to questions and key points brought out during the discussion will make you look thoughtful and committed. If you find that 15 minutes into the conversation, you haven't taken a single note, just write as few words down to make it look like you're taking notes. Remember: It's all about perception. However, it's important to jot down key points discussed during the interview, as they can prompt you during the final moments of the conversation. Recalling significant particulars of the discussion will demonstrate to the interviewer that you were carefully following what was being said and will allow you to spin the interview to position you in the most positive and memorable light.

Before You Depart the Interview

Finally, before you leave, if you want the job, it's perfectly appropriate to say so ("Mr. Smith, I not only appreciated the opportunity to speak with you, but also how our conversation confirmed my initial feelings about the position. I feel this would be a great place at which to work and I thank you for your consideration.").

Something to ponder: An innovative and memorable question to ask before the end of the conversation might be to inquire if there is anything discussed that needs more clarification or elaboration. Quite often, this will allow you the opportunity to correct and/or clarify an issue that might have been an offer-derailer.

Thank Yous

Everybody tells you to follow-up after a job interview; do you know what most job candidates do? They send a thank you-email. Instead, I strongly suggest that you send a handwritten thank-you note following an interview (as opposed to an e-mail). A handwritten note says you took the time to put pen to paper, and will make you stand out. My suggestion is to be strategic and write the note *before* the interview, stamp it, and address it, and put it in the mail immediately following the meeting. Years ago, when I was putting together a selling skills program for Janssen Pharmaceuticals, I brought a district manager in from the field to help spearhead the pilot program. Following the rotation, he was the only one to write me a handwritten thank-you note, which I immediately showed the company president. Today, this individual is the CEO of one of the largest and most well-known companies in the world. I can say with authority that his rise in business can be directly tied to his ability to forge relationships through little things like handwritten notes of appreciation. Use the "etiquette advantage" and always send a thank-you note! This is important not just for the sake of good manners, but to set you apart and make you more memorable.

Follow Up

If one week has gone by and you haven't gotten any word, reach out to the office of the interviewer and ask about the status of the position. If the job is still open, this is an ideal time to let them know that you are available and interested in the job. Enthusiasm is really important, as I've found that often, the most enthusiastic applicants are chosen out of a pool of evenly qualified individuals.

When I began this chapter, I mentioned that there are many interviews that you experience, almost daily, that are not related to job-hunting—like an annual review ("Tell me how you feel you've carried out your professional development objectives.") or an unexpected encounter in the company cafeteria with the big boss ("So, what's this new digital marketing project I've heard so much about? How is it going?"). Many of the same rules apply. You never know when a 30-second "elevator speech" on any subject may come in handy. Be prepared to deliver them with the tools suggested here and you will be amazed how others will be more disposed to hire you, impressed by you, find you credible, believe what you say, and do what you want them to do.

In summary, if you want to survive and actually succeed in our Snapshot Society, with its ever-narrowing window of opportunity, you must literally embody the benefits you bring. Personal packaging, facial engagement, energy, visceral contact, and follow-up all add up to Executive Presence—defined as a most exclusive state of existing—designed to impress and connect. Regardless of the subject of the interview, don't forget, it never really ends. As I said in the Preface, "Buy from me, date me, elect me, promote me." Hire me!

Face-to-face encounters are becoming more and more a rarity. When you are lucky enough to engage live with someone, don't squander the opportunity! Follow this guide; it's how you'll succeed when seconds don't allow for second chances.

? Test Yourself!

1.	What can an interview accomplish that a resume/application cannot?
2.	Why is it not a good idea to wear a new outfit to an interview?
3.	What is the importance of facial engagement?
4.	How can a poor handshake ruin an interview?
5.	Why is it a good idea to discuss the hiring time line?
6.	What are the advantages of a handwritten thank you?
7.	What kind of questions should you prepare before an interview?

Epilogue

Clearing the Way

To realize that you do not understand is a virtue; not to realize that you do not understand is a defect.

—Lao Tzu

Mission Statement
Perception is the key to your success—both in the acting and the asking.

New York City lies about 1,200 miles from Michigan, where, as you know, I grew up and went to college. By current accepted wisdom, my adopted hometown, New York, is considered the center of business and culture in the Western world. It has more theaters, museums, corporate headquarters, and high-end shopping per square mile than any other city in any other country on Earth. Because of its history, or maybe in spite of it, New York is also the number-one high-value target for job-seekers looking for an opportunity in finance, business, entertainment, the arts, fashion, advertising, cable TV, sports, food services, and hospitality. New York, New York: It really is the city so nice they named it twice. And for good reason.

But like all good things, there's also a downside: New York can be a cold, unforgiving, unpredictable, often-inhospitable landscape in which even good deeds are frowned upon, and the laws of cause and effect go out the window quicker than the Naked Cowboy's pants come off in Times Square.

I spent the formative years of my professional life working for others as on-air talent in TV news, as a congressional speechwriter, as a buyer at retail, working in public relations, and as a senior executive and member of the executive committee at a Fortune 500 company. I've spent the bulk of my working career running my own business as a media, PR, and strategic consultant to a wide range of mostly interesting, sometimes-terrifying, never-dull movers and shakers; captains of industry, many of whom have senior roles in corporations all over the globe. Some of my clients even run those companies. Somehow, I've also found time to speak at upward of 200 live events a year and still managed to build a family with my husband, David, and daughter, Avery.

With all of my life experience, if there's one thing I've learned it's that no matter what you think, perception is reality. So the first thing you must learn, or re-learn, or let seep into your consciousness as we launch you into implementing your ultimate success plan is this: It's not always what you do that counts the most; it's how what you do lands on others. The funny thing is I didn't learn this lesson in the boardrooms and grand ballrooms that have occupied so much of my time these past 20 years. I learned it on a New York City cross-town bus.

The fall day was cold and the air held the kind of crispness you might smell in a small-town apple orchard. Even though this is the big city, there are still subtle nuances about it that can surprise and delight, like smelling fresh cider on a city street corner in late fall. For those who don't know, Manhattan is laid out like a big banana, roughly 3 miles wide and 8 miles long. The famous avenues, 5th Ave, Madison Avenue, Park Avenue, Broadway, and so on, run uptown and downtown, and are crisscrossed by its famous streets: 57th Street, 42nd Street, 34th Street, and 14th Street, in a seemingly endless patchwork quilt of cars, pedestrians, cabs, and above ground mass transit that knows no equal. One morning, not long after I changed my life again and relocated to the city to begin my third or fourth career—this one in public relations—I got on the 57th Street cross-town bus.

In New York, all classes of people take public transportation and that day was no exception. Even if you have a pile of cash, one of the best ways to commute comfortably and inexpensively from New York's Upper East Side (a bastion of well-heeled apartment buildings and well-to-do upper-middle-class families) is to take the bus from the East Side across town into the heart of the business district.

On this day I got on the bus, winded and ready for a nap, and my work-day hadn't even begun! Sitting across from me, two aisles away, was a nice-looking, rather affluent older man wearing a tailored suit and a large gold Rolex watch planted firmly on his left wrist. He was sitting alone. I remember traffic was light and the bus was less than half full. A stop or two after I got on, a couple of young toughs came on board and sat opposite the guy with the Rolex. It didn't take long for me to see these guys were looking at the man like two half-starved predators sizing up their prey.

The older man stood up. Maybe his was the next stop, or perhaps he just had a feeling standing was the right thing to do, or in this case the wrong thing to do. As soon as Rolex man entered the aisle, one of the young thugs got in front of the man and backed into him. As he did, the other thug came from behind, reached into the older gent's pocket, and snatched his wallet. Lucky me, all this was happening right in front of my face. With almost no regard for life or limb (okay, so that's a little dramatic) I began hitting the hand of the predator who had just grabbed the wallet.

I jumped out of my seat and started slapping the mugger's hand with my purse. I'll tell you, the memory of the look on that guy's face, even today, is priceless. He couldn't believe this young girl was attacking him with her handbag and yelling with such ferocity that the driver was forced to stop the bus and open the doors. The robbers assessed the situation and without further drama bolted from the bus, one from the front door, the other from the rear. The bus lurched forward and, as it did, I almost fell onto my perfectly pleated rear end. As I hung on for dear life, I could see the two goons now on the street running after the bus, arms pumping, four letter words flying, threats mixing with angry spittle, but I didn't care one bit. I was a hero. *I was a hero!*

I turned back, reached down, picked up the wallet, and handed it to the Rolex-wearing gent who hardly seemed to notice that his wallet and possibly his watch were the targets of brazen mid-town robbers. Without so much as a thank you, the man sat back in his seat, eyes forward. Well, so much for gratitude.

As I turned again to sit back down, a woman in her mid-60s behind me leaned closer. I thought, "Here it is," finally a little recognition for what I'd just done. "You had to get involved, didn't you?" she hissed, "bet you're pretty pleased, being a hero and all. Do you realize you've just ruined it for the rest of us? Shame on you, missy. Shame on you!"

I was confused.

"You heard me. Don't pretend you didn't. Now we're a target. Sure as we're sittin' here those idiots are comin' back and will seek revenge."

"Revenge," I thought, chilled by the idea of it. She continued.

"Mark my words. Who's next? Me? You? Him?" She nodded her head toward the thankless old guy. "Thanks for nothing. Next time that's exactly what you should do. Nothing!"

As if to emphasize her point she stood up, stabbed at me with her cane, and hobbled to the rear door. As she exited the bus, her facial expression said it all.

I thought I had just interrupted a brazen mid-morning robbery on a New York City bus, but it had turned into a misstep in the eyes of my co-rider who feared retribution for my actions. I was confused. More than that I was intrigued. How could something so right seem so wrong in the eyes of another?

That leads me to one of the key lessons from this book: If you're going to get recognized, rewarded, and promoted for the things you do, unless the people around you—your team, coworkers, and most importantly your superiors—opt into your actions and believe you're doing exactly the right thing at the right moment, then no matter what you do, it might never be good enough, or right enough, or recognized enough.

Because this is a book about thriving in a business environment it's important for you to realize that the effect you have on others is a factor than can influence your destiny. Sure, there are plenty of other ways to make a living that don't involve being in a company. But if your dream is to make it and succeed in the hallowed halls of the big and small, new and old infrastructures, the awareness and advice gleaned from *Your Ultimate Success Plan* will prove extremely useful.

It's never been a better, more thrilling time to work in a business environment that excites you and makes you happy, if not eager, to get out of bed in the morning. This is truly one of life's great pleasures. To be ensconced in a work place that holds no excitement, that bores you, terrifies you, makes you want to play hooky every day, or makes you want to quit and sing opera aboard a cruise ship, is a stultifying, oppressive condition that can actually lead to a host of bad things including anxiety, depression, overeating, undereating, nail biting, and the list goes on. If you've taken this book to heart, none of that is going to happen to you going forward, at least not without a big, juicy fight. So, here is my pledge to you: Together we've journeyed through a book (that I wrote and you're reading) dedicated to helping you thrive in a business setting, no matter what the size, and even more importantly, it's a book that gives you permission to remove the chains that have been holding you back from getting what you really want so you can "go for it" with more appropriate, helpful, and meaningful insights and strategies than ever before.

Let's uncouple the previously mentioned chains. I'm not referring to the kind of restraint that others place on you, but instead the self-imposed chains that prevent us from establishing a trajectory that makes sense and fulfills our deepest, most passionate goals. I said in the FAQs that if you got this book, or previewed this book, or someone loaned you this book, that there would be takeaways, helpful tidbits or useable insights on almost every page that could help you right away. So let's remind you of one right now. At least for the moment, forget all about being recognized, rewarded, and promoted. Forget about the outcome. Instead, think about what you dream about or love doing the most, whether it's your job or a hobby that has nothing to do with making money. It doesn't matter. It just has to be something you love so much that simply in the doing of it you feel successful.

Are you thinking? Good. Now, hold on to the notion that the first place success begins—the place where your ultimate success plan has to start if it's going to work—is inside of you! You don't need a boss or a coworker or your husband or girlfriend or your sous-chef to tell you what brings you joy; that's your territory, and who knows what you like better than you? Deal with it.

Here's another thought: You start being successful by feeling successful, and that process starts with you being the boss of you. Though that might seem like a bit of an oversimplification, it's not. The only way we're going to get others to buy into what you're selling is for you to believe in the product. In this case, the product is *you*! When you feel good and are motivated to do a great job, when you're doing something you like or love it's much easier for others to feel your passion and to believe in you.

Doing something you like to do is important. As famous piano man Billy Joel exclaimed, "If you are not doing what you love, you are wasting your time."[2]

Face it: It's much easier to get out of bed on a rainy morning and make the commute into work when you're excited about what you're doing. It's estimated that somewhere between 20 to 30 percent of our work life is spent getting to and from the office. There have been times in my life when I've spent more hours commuting than I did with my family. Ouch. Traveling can be exhausting and everyday commuting is one of the struggles we face as some of us live in metro areas where being close to the office often means it's too expensive to live there. There's no doubt commuting can take more time and energy than you'd like, so by the time you get to work you're already hungry, tired, and looking for a break. Do that for 15 to 20 years, over and over, and tell me how you feel.

Amy Poehler, the wonderful actor and comedienne, writes in her memoir: "Creativity is connected to your passion, that light that drives you. Career is different. Career is the stringing together of opportunities and jobs...career is the thing that will not fill you up and never make you truly whole."[3] In short, the quickest way to build or re-build the new independent state of you is to focus on your passion and then maybe, if you're like many who've come before, career success will follow. It can happen. I've seen it. What gets in the way more than the cranky boss or the crummy coworker, more than the demanding spouse or distracting kids, is you. And that's what we're aiming to change.

As Gretchen Rubin, best-selling author of *The Happiness Project* admonishes, "So, if there's something that you wish you did more regularly, try doing it every day. Write every day, pack a lunch every day, go for a walk every day, read every day. It's easier!"[4]

In order to be recognized, rewarded, and promoted (now we've got our sights eagerly set on outcome) within large and small companies alike, you not only have to think and act differently in an ever-changing landscape, you also have to step up your game by shedding behaviors that no longer serve you!

Here's another takeaway; this one's a bit harder to see in ourselves but easy to see in others: We live in a reactive world, where most people tend to deal with specific events and circumstances with conditioned behaviors that yield only short-term benefits and negative long-term consequences.

People take action in response to constriction or deficit, and if done often enough wonder why the corner office isn't looming large in their legend. The answer isn't an enigma wrapped in a mystery. It's quite clear! These limiting behaviors simply don't work.

Consider that sometimes it is way better to keep your eyes open and your mouth shut! You want to be relevant; looking for and responding to the non-verbal cues of others are critical. So is the need to be memorable. Translation: "Think long and talk short." Distill in your head, do the silent drill down, and deliver information that's digestible, value-added, and relatable. Your job isn't to succumb to the "curse of knowledge," as described in the popular tomb *Made to Stick,* in which authors Chip and Dan Heath examine how unsuccessful people "bury the lead." They assert that these hapless subjects make themselves forgettable and then wonder why peers, superiors, and subordinates don't act on their information.[5] This concept is a foundational cornerstone of my keynotes. I peel back this phenomenon in my workshops as well, using a common comparator to illustrate the point how effective communicating is like packing a Travel Pro versus a steamer trunk. The small carry-on roller bag requires purposeful editing: When space is at a premium, you take just what you need for your trip, versus the steamer trunk, which encourages you to pack any and everything, regardless of whether you'll actually wear it or not. The result is that you literally haul around excess baggage that ruins the trip, tires you out, and even costs you money, as you can't possibly carry it yourself and are constantly tipping others to transport it.

If you routinely find yourself over-talking, revisit your mission. Are you trying to telegraph how smart you are (which no one cares about) or how right you are (which, depending on benefits, makes people care a lot)?

Although it's important to get to the point, it's also important to make your point and ask for what you need, want, or deserve.

Don't Be Afraid to Ask

How we get "stuff" (goods, services, favors, relationships, help, promotions, assets—you name it) occupies much of our thoughts and deeds each and every day. For the most part, "stuff" doesn't just fall into our laps; we have to ask! As mentioned in the Preface, we all want people to buy from us, date us, elect us and promote us, but the sad truth is that for many, the "ask" is very difficult. This begs the question: Why is it so hard for us to ask for the things we so desperately need, want, and, in most cases, deserve?

Regardless of how we communicate, face-to-face, verbally, and digitally, the ask is relatively complex. There are many kinds of asks: a favor ("Could I borrow your car this evening?"), a demand ("I am asking everyone to be here by 6 p.m. sharp!"), a negotiation ("Will you give me a discount if I pay in cash?"), advice ("Will you please think about what I've told you?"), even a statement disguised as an ask ("Do you believe she actually walked out of the house in that outfit?"). The hardest asks are those that are perceived as giving power to the "grantor" because, unless they agree, you cannot move forward. So, depending on the level of importance, we must go through a sequenced process leading up to the ask in order to increase the chances of a yes:

1. We ingratiate to make sure the grantor thinks positively about us.

2. We figure out a way to lead into discussing the situation that requires the ask.

3. We (sometimes nervously) narrate the scenario that creates the need.

4. We get to the actual ask, but we're not done yet.

5. We follow up the ask with a modifier that makes it okay if the answer is no ("Look, I understand if you can't do this, but...").

This is an extremely stressful procedure that requires us to go through all sorts of mental and ego gyrations, analysis, and preparation in order to feel confident enough to go for it. We initially approach the individual whom we think presents the best odds of saying yes; unless it's an emergency, we play down the need in order to avoid looking too desperate, we ask for the absolute minimum so the grantor doesn't think he or she has to give too much, and we make the ask optional so the potential grantor doesn't feel bad if they have to refuse. Whew!

It was in 1933, at the depth of the Great Depression, that Franklin D. Roosevelt, in his first inaugural address, quoted the immortal line "The only thing we have to fear is fear itself."[6] But it is that very thing, fear, that stops so many of us from the ask. What is that fear? Quite simply, we will do anything to avoid hearing the word no! Remember our examination of *Go for No* in Chapter 10? For most people, *no* is the poster-word for rejection and, for most of us, rejection is intolerable. Rejection has a tendency to bring out the worst in us—shame, fear, and a paralysis that floods our thoughts with fury, while at the same time, eats away at our self-confidence and esteem. It threatens our whole feeling of being part of something greater than ourselves. Much has been researched on this subject, especially the activity of the brain when one experiences rejection. Not surprisingly, what was discovered is that when we're rejected, the same parts of the brain get activated as when we experience real pain. The two reactions are so linked to each other that when scientists gave participants in a study Tylenol before subjecting them to a rejection experiment, they said they experienced much less emotional distress than the group who wasn't given the pain reliever. Go figure.

If you ever followed the once-popular television series *Survivor* you will note the expression of pain on the individual's face when they were voted off the island. It was like a stab in the chest; no wonder we'll do anything to avoid that feeling.

But here's the thing. It's not about *Getting to Yes*, the title of the self-help book on successfully negotiating; it's about living with, responding to, and overcoming *no*. It's what the experts say stretches you and what popular author Carol Dweck asserts encourages a "growth mindset," as a key factor in the new psychology of success.[7]

Presumably, one asks for something he or she doesn't currently have (a raise, someone's vote, a date). If you ask and are denied, then you are no worse off than you were before you made your request! It's not like "I won't go out with you (and by the way I'm going to tell everyone else not to go out with you either!)." The only one who punishes us when we hear *no* is ourselves, and managing that expectation will allow you to not only get over the initial issue of being rejected, but will also determine how you come back and ask again.

One of my favorite stories regarding how to deal with the fear of rejection and hearing the dreaded no was published in *O Magazine* some years ago. Successful author Suzanne Finnamore wrote about an incident early in her career in advertising. In order to curry favor with her boss and attend a fancy company trip to Maui, she prepared a massive presentation for their client. Although the presentation went very well, it wasn't enough to impress her boss, who informed Suzanne she would in fact be staying behind. Instead of being dejected, Ms. Finnamore turned staying behind into an uninterrupted opportunity to revise her resume and send it to a large agency in San Francisco.

Her timing was perfect. Within days, she had secured an interview and an offer! She gave her two-week notice and never looked back. This two-time winner of the Oprah Book Club Pick advises, "Don't just get even—go to a much higher place where they can't see you from their lawn chairs, which are probably missing slats."[8]

What Suzanne did was depersonalize and then strategize. She didn't personalize the situation; she simply realized that her efforts weren't being appreciated and, in order for her to feel whole, she needed to move on. With that confidence, she was able to ask for something even greater than what she had—refusing to engage in the self-defeating process of trying to figure out why her boss didn't like her. In short, it's imperative that you put your efforts into things you can control, and avoid wasting time and emotional capital on things you can't control.

More and more, I find when conducting workshops, attendees always bring technology backup, often in several forms, such as smartphones, iPads, and laptops. Everyone thinks they can multitask, so during my overview, they take advantage of being able to listen to me while checking e-mails. Initially, while finding this somewhat disconcerting, I used to allow participants to keep their laptops open, check messages, and swish through applications. I thought if I said anything, and asked them to unplug, they would get mad and disengage. Well, eventually I realized that this was not going to work. Multi-tasking is an oxymoron; you can't really do two things well at the same time. So I had tough choices. I could risk their ire by asking them to shut off their technology or deal with the distraction by jumping around like a circus clown to get their ongoing attention. The latter was exhausting and demeaning, so that was out, and I came up with a better strategy. I would announce at the beginning of the session that I was asking everyone to shut down their computers and turn off their smartphones. In return, I would give them all ample break time to check messages and return calls. To maximize the time together, it was imperative that we would give each other our undivided attention. As part of the ask, I gave them a clear benefit, and it worked! As a result, I am rarely upstaged by an individual's technology, and participants find the unplugging refreshing! If I had been overly concerned with how the attendees would feel about me, and fail to ask for what I needed, I would have been unable to overcome the inevitable distractions that the devices provided. Like Ms. Finnamore, I depersonalized and strategized. This empowered me to go for the ask.

Never again will your default reaction be "If I ask, they might say no, and that would be intolerable!" Use the skills discussed in this book to empower you to declare, "If they say no, then I'll figure out an alternative and maybe get more than I initially asked for."

A key determining factor that will influence your behavior choices, one that you can put into practice immediately upon finishing this book, and in the very doing of it might begin your transformation sooner than you think is: Keep your eyes on the prize at all times!

What this means is, you don't have to be right, loud, proud, reactive, or mean. You don't have to play the role of victim, aggressor, wounded warrior, busy girl, or bossy boy if it means you're being negatively affected by your actions. Keep in mind that losing your cool doesn't mean you're effective. It actually means you're out of power, and that's a no-no in the eyes of your superiors. Knowing what you want, say the opportunity to present at your company's offsite retreat in a month, which has been denied, may or may not be tied to an office blowup that seemed innocent to you, but enough people complained and the higher ups put you in the penalty box without ever telling you. Your only clue that something is wrong; you didn't get to present at the offsite. By keeping your eyes on the bigger picture you might have to modulate and temper your reaction to things in the office, which will make you a more balanced, more engaged participant at work.

Don't be afraid to ask for feedback. If your rising star starts to stall, seek input and get to the source of the derailer; if you sense a negative change, ask for an explanation. A case in point: A brilliant female CEO for whom I provide executive coaching recently shared her "teachable moment." Fast-tracked at a Fortune 50 Company, she suddenly found herself not being invited to key client meetings and passed over for important presentations. She decided to confront what she sensed was a sea change in management's attitude toward her and was told she was too overly competitive with her peers—that her drive needed to be directed externally, not internally. Though she valued the feedback, took it to heart, and began to modify her behavior, this successful executive left the company soon after—not because of the constructive feedback (she actually benefitted from it) but because management was not transparent enough to volunteer it in the first place! It's this fearless and frank persona that now lets her lead an organization of 8,500 employees.

Clearly these qualities are admired by the higher ups, and the cause and effect of seeming to have your act together might not instantly translate into a reward or promotion, but it will start you down (actually up) the path to recognition—reward and promotion.

For much of my adult life I've coached professionals at all levels from myriad companies who have struggled with their careers. Stuck in jobs they didn't enjoy, many had to leave their workplace with no clear-cut plan how they would survive and thrive. That doesn't have to happen to you! You've read the book. Consider this your Independence Day where you can control and will modulate the desired outcomes of your actions, on your terms, by applying tactics and mid-course corrections that really work.

Let's celebrate the emergence of a new you, similar in many ways to the older, less-wise you. But now the new you *is* willing to take a hard look at the choices that define your progress on a daily basis.

Here's an exercise I like to offer some of my clients: Draw a line down the middle of one sheet of paper. Write on the left side all the things that happened today that didn't go well, in your eyes. This can be anything from a conversation that didn't go as planned to meeting times veering wildly from your calendar. On the right side, write down what went well: a good sales call, a conversation that might generate more business—overall, the victories large and small that made the day productive and worth remembering. You don't have to do anything other than be aware at this stage.

Although many items might land on the left side, with enhanced awareness from *Your Ultimate Success Plan*, you'll begin to address patterns that in no time will transform your sheet of paper into a right-column masterpiece. But, please don't think life is always going to give you what you want when you want it. That's not realistic, and where's the fun in that? Instead, you've already begun to cultivate a new situational awareness. Light-bulb moment! You're getting in touch with the idea that you can follow your passion and that you must be aware of self-limiting behaviors so you can make way for more of the good—clear away the underbrush and create a focused and purposeful path to getting *recognized, rewarded, and promoted.*

Notes

Preface
1. Eliot, "The Love Song," 10.
2. Allen, "The Early Essays," 107.

Introduction
1. Kelly, *Pogo*.
2. Twain, *What Is Man?*, 17.
3. Farmer and Shepherd-Wynn, *Voices of Historical*, 294.
4. Thoreau, *Walden*, 427.

Chapter 1
1. Kozlowski, "Biologist Richard Dawkins."
2. Wilde, BrainyQuote.com.
3. Dyer, *Excuses Begone!*, 44.
4. Price, *The Quotable Billionaire*, 20.
5. Goldman, *Adventures in the Screen Trade*, 39.
6. Carnegie, *How to Stop*, 219.
7. Kendrick, *Identifying and Managing*, 335.
8. Covey, *The Seven Habits*, 26, 98.
9. Ibid.

Chapter 2

1. Seuss, *Happy Birthday*, 44.
2. "The 16 Best Things Warren Buffett Has Ever Said." *The Huffington Post*, August 30, 2013.
3. Grisham, BrainyQuote.com.
4. "Tiffany & Co. Company History."
5. Kiefer, "At People Express."
6. Ibid.
7. Ibid.
8. Barron, "Low Airfares."
9. Dallos, "People Express."
10. Kiefer, "At People Express."
11. Kochneff, "The Rise and Fall."
12. Trumbore, "Discount Retailers."
13. Ibid.
14. Sobel, *When Giants Stumble*.
15. Trumbore, "Discount Retailers."
16. Medavoy and Young, *You're Only as Good*.
17. Associated Press. "Top Stars Join Orion Pictures," 10-A.
18. Ramirez, "Business People."
19. Tzioumakis, *American Independent Cinema,* 228–229.
20. Stevenson, "The Media Business.
21. Weiner, "MGM Ends Orion Orbit."
22. Peters, "The Brand Called You."
23. Faeth, "6 Inbound Marketing Lessons."

Chapter 3

1. Marx, *Goldwyn: A Biography,* 19.
2. Kinnes, "The ATU System."
3. Dowling, *The Cinderella Complex*.
4. Homer and Fagles, *The Odyssey*.
5. Horn, "Interview With Jake Gyllenhaal."
6. Hartman, *Tell Me a Joke, Please*, 97.
7. Andrews, *The Columbia Dictionary of Quotations*, 95.
8. Zimmerman, "The Problem with Pointing Fingers."
9. Ibid.

10. Ibid.
11. Ibid.
12. Price, *The Quotable Billionaire*, 20.

Chapter 4

1. Salzmann, *Alcott to Zaharias*, 17.
2. Santillano, "Don't Be Sorry."
3. Ibid.
4. McPhail, *Global Communication*, 90.
5. Rao, "Paula Deen."
6. Schumann and Ross, "Why Women Apologize," 1649–1655.
7. Ibid.
8. Singh, *Quote Unquote*, 28.
9. Turner, "How to Offer Apologies."
10. Green, "Where Is Dick Fuld Now?"

Chapter 5

1. Bedrij, *Exodus III*, 182.
2. Watkins, *Where's My Dog?*, 14.
3. Huppke, "Liar, Liar, Officepants on Fire."
4. Carter, *The Quotable Will Rogers*, 53.
5. Roosevelt, "Dedication by Radio."
6. Winokur, *Return of the Portable Curmudgeon*, 106.
7. CNN, "Great Lines from '60 Minutes.'"
8. Roberts and Wood, *Intellectual Virtues*.

Chapter 6

1. Hesse, *Siddhartha*, 163.

Chapter 7

1. Holtz, Boardofwisdom.com.
2. *The Devil Wears Prada*. Directed by David Frankel. New York: Twentieth Century Fox Film Corporation, 2006.
3. Angelou, *Wouldn't Take Nothing*.

Chapter 8

1. Roosevelt, T. "International Peace."
2. Byrne, "How Al Dunlap Self-Destructed."

3. Hogh, "Aggression at Work," 61.
4. Sandberg, *Nightline*.
5. Tichy and Charan, "Speed, Simplicity, Self-Confidence."
6. Marcus, "Best Advice."
7. Lewis, "Madonna Quotes."
8. Branson, "Richard Branson."
9. Hadfield and Hasson, *How to Be Assertive,* 12.
10. Farrell, "News: Being Assertive."
11. Myatt, *Leadership Matters,* 117.
12. Fisher, "No Satyla Nadella."

Chapter 9
1. Bullock, BrainyQuote.com.
2. Blanchard and Blanchard, "The 5 Biggest Mistakes."
3. Ibid.
4. Hess, "Don't Let Burning Bridges."

Chapter 10
1. Wilde, BrainyQuote.com.
2. Zetlin, "4 Reasons You Should."
3. Medvec, "New Connected Leadership."
4. Ibid.
5. Smith, "The New Connected Leadership."
6. Barra, "The New Connected Leadership."
7. Ludden, "Ask for a Raise?"
8. Ibid.
9. Fisher, "No Satyla Nadella."
10. Ibid.
11. Ibid.
12. Arquette, 87th Academy Awards speech.
13. Flynn and Lake, "If You Need Help," 128.
14. Lareau, *Unequal Childhoods*.
15. Baer, "Here's Why You Should."

Chapter 11
1. Covey, *The Seven Habits of Highly*, 98.
2. Lore, *The Pathfinder: How to Choose*, 14.
3. Warrell, "Afraid of Being."

4. Jehangir, Kareem, Khan, Muhammad, and Soherwardi. "Effects of Job Stress," 453.

5. Schlesinger, Kiefer, and Brown, *Just Start, Take Action.*

6. Coleman, Gulati, and Segovia, *Passion and Purpose.*

7. Ibid.

8. Rath, *Strengths Finder 2.0.*

9. Holland, "The Proverbial Ladder."

10. Mycoskie, *Start Something That Matters.*

11. Gallo, "Don't Like Your Job?"

12. Ibid.

13. Weinberg, "The Complainers."

14. Gallo, "Don't Like Your Job?"

Chapter 12

1. Ziglar, Ziglar.com.

2. Mehrabian, *Silent Messages.*

3. Gladwell, "Blink."

4. Bernieri, "Personality Perception."

5. Gorman, "Seven Seconds."

6. Biography of Hatesheput, accessed February 25, 2015. *www.biography.com/people/hatshepsut-9331094.*

7. Evans, "Eye Tracking Resume Study."

8. Giang, "What Recruiters Look at."

9. Cenendella, "Your Cover Letter."

10. Gladwell, "Blink Q & A."

Chapter 13

1. Curie, BrainyQuote.com.

2. Bryant and Jonsen, "Cross-Cultural Leadership."

3. Ibid.

4. Hofstede, "National Cultures in Four Dimensions."

5. Heim, *Hardball for Women.*

6. "Women 'Take Care,' Men 'Take Charge:' Catalyst.org, Catalyst, 2005. *www.catalyst.org/system/files/Women_Take_Care_Men_Take_Charge_Stereotyping_of_U.S._Business_Leaders_Exposed.pdf.*

7. "Different Cultures, Similar Perceptions."

8. Sawyer, "The Impact of New Social Media," 242.

9. Stelzner, "2013 Social Media Marketing Industry Report."

Chapter 14

1. Eliot, "The Love Song," 10.
2. *All That Jazz*.
3. Fiske, Cuddy, and Glick, "Universal Dimension."
4. Showalter, *Underdog Edge*, 39.
5. Sullivan, *1000 Ways to Recruit Top Talent*.

Epilogue

1. Tzu, BrainyQuote.com
2. Joel. BrainyQuote.com.
3. Poehler, *Yes Please*.
4. Rubin, *The Happiness Project*.
5. Heath and Heath, *Made to Stick*.
6. Roosevelt, Inaugural Address.
7. Dweck, *Mindset: The Psychology of Success*.
8. Finnamore, "Found Success."

Bibliography

All That Jazz, directed by Bob Fosse. Century City, Calif.: 20th Century Fox, 1979.

Allen, Woody. "The Early Essays," in *Without Feathers*. New York: Ballantine Books, 1975.

Andrews, Robert. *The Columbia Dictionary of Quotations*. New York: Columbia University Press, 1993.

Angelou, Maya. *Wouldn't Take Nothing for My Journey Now*. Toronto: Random House of Canada, 1993.

Arquette, Patricia. 87th Academy Awards speech, Hollywood, Calif. February 22, 2015.

Associated Press. "Top Stars Join Orion Pictures." *Wilmington Morning Star* (November 22, 1978; page 10-A). Retrieved November 2, 2011.

Baer, Drake. "Here's Why You Should Always Make The First Offer in a Negotiation." *Business Insider*, May 14, 2014. *www.businessinsider. com/how-to-negotiate-make-first-offer-2014-5*.

Barra, Mary. "The New Connected Leadership." Panel discussion at the 2014 Fortune Magazine's Most Powerful Women Summit, October 6–8, 2014.

Barron, James. "Low Airfares in East Changing Travel Habits and Business Plans." *New York Times*, December 25, 1984. *www.nytimes. com/1984/12/25/us/low-air-fares-in-east-changing-travel-habits-and-business-plans.html*, accessed February 25, 2015.

Bedrij, Orest. *Exodus III: Great Joy and Glory to the Most High as You*. Bloomington, Ind.: Xlibris Corporation, 2011.

Bernieri, Frank. "Personality perception: a Developmental Study," in *Journal of Research in Personality*, 40 (5): 2006.

Blanchard, Ken, and Scott Blanchard. "The 5 Biggest Mistakes You're Making with Work Relationships." *Fast Company*, April 23, 2012. *www.fastcompany. com/1834912/5-biggest-mistakes-youre-making-work-relationships*.

Boice, Trina. *My Future's So Bright I Gotta Wear Shades*. Springville, Utah: CFI, 2014.

Branson, Richard. "Richard Branson: Nice Guys Can Finish First." Entrepreneur.com, 2010. *www.entrepreneur.com/article/217309*.

Bryant, Ben, and Karsten Jonsen. "Cross-Cultural Leadership: How to run operations in markets we don't understand," October 2008. *www. imd.org/research/challenges/TC082-08.cfm*.

Bullock, Sandra. BrainyQuote.com, Xplore Inc, 2015 *www.brainyquote.com/ quotes/quotes/s/sandrabull336260.html*, accessed February 23, 2015.

Byrne, John A. "How Al Dunlap Self-Destructed." *BusinessWeek*, July 6 1998. *www.businessweek.com/1998/27/b3585090.htm*.

Carnegie, Dale. *How to Stop Worrying and Start Living*. New York: Pocket Books, 1990.

Carter, Joseph H. *The Quotable Will Rogers*. Layton, Utah: Gibbs Smith, 2005.

Cenendella, Mark. "Your Cover Letter Is Too Long." TheLadders. com, 2013. *www.theladders.com/career-newsletters/ your-cover-letter-is-too-long*.

Clifton, Donald O., and Tom Rath. *Strengths Finder 2.0*, 2007.

CNN. "Great Lines from '60 Minutes' Commentator Andy Rooney" CNN. com, 5 November 2011, *www.cnn.com/2011/11/05/showbiz/andy-rooney-quotes/*, accessed February 24, 2015.

Coleman, John, Daniel Gulati, and W.O. Segovia. *Passion and Purpose: Stories from the Best and Brightest Young Business Leaders*. Boston: Harvard Business Review Press, 2011.

Covey, Stephen R. *The Seven Habits of Highly Effective People*. New York: Simon & Schuster, 1989.

Curie, Marie. BrainyQuote.com, Xplore Inc, accessed February 23, 2015. *www.brainyquote.com/quotes/quotes/m/mariecurie389010.html*.

Dallos, Robert. "People Express, Frontier Unit Slash Air Fares: Subsidiary Will Become Discount, No-Frills Line" *Los Angeles Times*,

February 11, 1986. *http://articles.latimes.com/1986-02-11/business/ fi-23001_1_frontier-airlines,* accessed February 25, 2015

Dattner, Ben. *The Blame Game: How the Hidden Rules of Credit and Blame Determine Our Success or Failure.* New York: Free Press, 2011.

Devil Wears Prada, The. Directed by David Frankel. 2006. New York: Twentieth Century Fox Film Corporation, 2006.

"Different Cultures, Similar Perceptions: Stereotyping Western European Business Leaders." Catalysit.org. Catalyst, 2006. *www.catalyst. org/system/files/ Different_Cultures%2C_Similar_Perceptions_ Stereotyping_of_Western_European_Business_Leaders.pdf.*

Dowling, Colette. *The Cinderella Complex.* New York: Pocket Books, 1982.

Dweck, Carol. *Mindset: The Psychology of Success.* New York: Ballantine Books, 2007.

Dundes, Alan, ed. *Cinderella: A Casebook.* Madison: University of Wisconsin Press, 1988.

Dyer, Wayne W. *Excuses Begone! How to Change Lifelong, Self-Defeating Thinking Habits.* Carlsbad, Calif.: Hay House, 2009.

Eliot, T.S. "The Love Song of J. Alfred Prufrock," in *The Waste Land, Prufrock and Other Poems.* Stilwell, Kansas: Digireads.com Publishing, 2005.

Evans, Will. "Eye Tracking Resume Study." TheLadders.com, 21 March 2012. *http://cdn.theladders.net/static/images/basicSite/pdfs/ TheLadders-EyeTracking-StudyC2.pdf.*

Faeth, Bill. "6 Inbound Marketing Lessons from David Ogilvy." *Business 2 Community,* 4 November 2013, *www.business2community.com/ marketing/6-inbound-marketing-lessons-david-ogilvy-0663664,* accessed February 24, 2015.

Farmer, Vernon L., and Evelyn Shepherd-Wynn. *Voices of Historical and Contemporary Black American Pioneers. Law and Government.* Santa Barbara, Calif.: ABC-CLIO, LLC, 2012.

Farrell, Robyn. "News: Being Assertive in the Workplace." *First For Women Insurance Company,* accessed February 23, 2015, *www. firstforwomen.co.za/being-assertive-in-the-workplace/.*

Finnamore, Suzanne. "Found Success." Wildmountainmemoir. wordpress.com. 4 January 2013. *https:// wildmountainmemoir.wordpress.com/2013/01/04/ retreat-faculty-suzanne-finnamore-on-overcoming-rejection/.*

Fisher, Anne. "No Satyla Nadella, You Can't Count on 'Karma' to Get You a Pay Raise." *Fortune Magazine*, October 10, 2014. *http://fortune.com/2014/10/10/women-pay-satya-nadella-microsoft/*.

Fiske, Susan T., Amy J. Cuddy, and Peter Glick, "Universal Dimension of Social Cognition: Warmth and Competence," *Trends in Cognitive Science*, 11 February 2007.

Flora, Carlin . "The Once-Over." *PsychologyToday.com*. 1 May 2004. *www.psychologytoday.com/articles/200407/the-once-over*.

Flynn, Francis, J. and Vanessa KB Lake. "If you need help, just ask: underestimating compliance with direct requests for help," *Journal of Personality and Psychology* 95.1 (2008): 128.

Gallo, Amy. "Don't Like Your Job? Change It (Without Quitting)," *Harvard Business Review*, 19 June 2012, online edition, *https://hbr.org/2012/06/dont-like-your-job-change-it-w*, accessed February 23, 2015.

Giang, Vivian. "What Recruiters Look at During the 6 Seconds They Spend on Your Resume." *BusinessInsider.com*, 9 April 2012. *www.businessinsider.com/heres'what-recruiters-look-at-suring-the-6-seconds-they-spend-on-your-resume-2012-4*

Gladwell, Malcolm. "Blink Q & A with Malcolm." Gladwell.com, accessed February 25, 2015. *http://gladwell.com/blink/blink-q-and-a-with-malcolm/*.

Goldman, William. *Adventures in the Screen Trade*. New York: Warner Books, 1983.

Gorman, Carol Kinsey. "Seven Seconds to Make a First Impression." Forbes.com. 13 February 2011. *www.forbes.com/sites/carolkinseygoman/2011/02/13/seven-seconds-to-make-a-first-impression*.

Green, Joshua. "Where is Dick Fuld Now?" September 12, 2013 Bloomberg–Businessweek, accessed February 25, 2015 *www.bloomberg.com/bw/articles/2013-09-12/where-is-dick-fuld-now-finding-lehman-brothers-last-ceo*

Grisham, John. BrainyQuote.com, Xplore Inc, 2015. *www.brainyquote.com/quotes/quotes/j/johngrisha418568.html*, accessed February 25, 2015.

Gutfeld, Greg. "Gutfeld: Hollywood Hypocrites Take On Equality." *Fox News*, 23 February 2015, *www.foxnews.com/on-air/the-five/article/2015/02/23/gutfeld-hollywood-hypocrites-take-equality*, accessed February 25, 2015.

Hadfield, Sue and Gill Hasson, *How to be Assertive in Any Situation*. U.K.: Pearson, Chapter one, 2010.

Hartman, Randy J. *Tell Me A Joke, Please: Humor for the Little Redneck in All of Us*. Bloomington, Ind.: iUniverse, 2009.

"Hatshepsut Biography." The Biography.com, accessed Feb 25, 2015. *www. biography.com/people/hatshepsut-9331094.*

Heath, Chip and Dan Heath. *Made to Stick*. New York: Random House, 2007.

Heim, Patricia. *Hardball for Women*: *Winning at the Game of Business*. New York: Plume, 1992.

Hess, Michael. "Don't Let Burning Bridges Fall on You." *CBS Moneywatch*, Interactive, Inc., 18 July 2012. *www.cbsnews.com/news/ dont-let-burning-bridges-fall-on-you/.*

Hesse, Hermann. *Siddhartha*. Cambridge, Mass.: Courier Corporation, 1998.

Hofstede, Geert. "National Cultures in Four Dimensions." TheHofstedeCentre.com, accessed March 23, 2015. *http://geert-hofstede.com/national-culture.html*

Hogh, Annie. "Aggression at Work: Bullying, Nasty Teasing and Violence. Prevalence, Mediating Factors and Consequences." Copenhagen: National Institute of Occupational Health, 2009. *www. arbejdsmiljoforskning.dk/upload/ah-phd.pdf.*

Holland, Stephanie. "The Proverbial Ladder: Are You Climbing The Right Wall?" *HuffingtonPost*, 26 July 2013, *www.huffingtonpost. co.uk/stephanie-holland/third-metric-success-the-proverbial-ladder_b_3627547.html.*

Holtz, Lou. Boardofwisdom.com, 2014. *http://boardofwisdom.com/togo/ Quotes/ShowQuote?msgid=14#.VOtH3HzF_nh*, accessed February 23, 2015.

Homer, and Robert Fagles. *The Odyssey*. New York: Penguin Classics, 1997.

Horn, Steven. "Interview with Jake Gyllenhaal." IGN.com, 28 May 2004, *www.ign.com/articles/2004/05/28/interview-with-jake-gyllenhaal*, accessed February 20, 2015.

Huffington Post." The 16 Best Things Warren Buffet Has Ever Said." *The Huffington Post*, last updated August 30, 2013. *www.huffingtonpost. com/2013/08/30/warren-buffett-quotes_n_3842509.html.* (quoting Warren Buffet).

Huppke, Rex. "Liar, Liar, Officepants on Fire." *Chicago Tribune*, 17 June 2013, *http://articles.chicagotribune.com/2013-06-17/business/ct-biz-0617-work-advice-huppke-20130617_1_white-lies-honesty-workplace*, accessed February 24, 2015.

Jehangir, Muhammad, Nasir Kareem, and Ayaz Khan, Muhammad Tahir Jan, and Shaheed Soherwardi. "Effects of Job Stress on Job Performance & Job Satisfaction." *Interdisciplinary Journal of Contemporary Research in Business* 3 (2011): 453.

Joel, Billy. BrainyQuote.com, Xplore Inc, 2015. *www.brainyquote.com/ quotes/quotes/b/ billyjoel383140.html*, accessed February 20, 2015.

Kelly, Walt (c). *Pogo*. April 1970. Post-Hall Syndicate.

Kendrick, Tom. *Identifying and Managing Project Risk*. New York: Amacom, 2009.

Kiefer, Francine. "At People Express, the Rush to Profits Never Slows Down" *Christian Science Monitor* December 19, 1983. *www.csmonitor.com/1983/1219/121916.html* accessed February 25, 2015.

Kinnes, T. "The ATU System." *AT Types of Folktales. http://oaks.nvg.org/ folktale-types.html*, accessed February 24, 2015.

Kochneff, Eric "The Rise and Fall of PEOPLExpress" Airliners.net, August 13, 2004. / *www.airliners.net/aviation-articles/read. main?id=68*, accessed February 25, 2015.

Korkki, Phyllis. "The True Calling That Wasn't" *New York Times*, 17 July 2010. *www.nytimes.com/2010/07/18/jobs/18search. html?_r=2&scp=1&sq=Nichlos%20Lore&st=cse&*

Kozlowski, Lori. "Biologist Richard Dawkins on the Evolution Debate," *Los Angeles Times*, 4 November 2009, *http://articles.latimes. com/2009/nov/04/news/la-sciw-dawkins-qanda4-2009nov04*, accessed February 20, 2015.

Lareau, Annette. *Unequal Childhoods: Class, Race, and Family Life*. Los Angeles: University of California Press, 2003.

Lewis, Jone Johnson. "Madonna Quotes." *About Women's History*. accessed Februrary 23, 2015, *http://womenshistory.about.com/od/quotes/a/ madonna.htm*.

Lore, Nicholas. *The Pathfinder: How to Choose or Change Your Career for a Lifetime of Satisfaction and Success*. New York: Simon & Schuster, 2012.

Ludden, Jennifer. "Ask For A Raise? Most Women Hesitate." *NPR*, February 8, 2011. *www.npr.org/2011/02/14/133599768/ ask-for-a-raise-most-women-hesitate*.

Marcus, David. "Best Advice." Linked In. accessed February 23, 2015. *www. linkedin.com/channels/best_advice*.

Marx, Arthur. *Goldwyn: A Biography of the Man Behind the Myth*. New York: W.W. Norton & Company, 1976.

McPhail, Thomas L. *Global Communication: Theories, Stakeholders and Trends*. United Kingdom: Wiley-Blackwell, 2010.

Medavoy, Mike and Young, Josh. *You're Only as Good as Your Next One: 100 Great Films, 100 Good Films, and 100 for Which I Should Be Shot*. New York: Atria Books, 2002.

Medvec, Victoria. "The New Connected Leadership." Panel discussion at the 2014 Fortune Magazine's Most Powerful Women Summit, October 6–8, 2014.

Mehrabian, Albert. *Silent Messages: Implicit Communication of Emotions and Attitudes*. Belmont, Calif.: Wadsworth, 1972.

Murphy, Jr., Bill. "30 Inspiring Quotes About Embracing Foolishness." Inc.com, 1 April 2014, *www.inc.com/bill-murphy-jr/30-inspiring-quotes-about-embracing-foolishness.html*, accessed February 24, 2015.

Myatt, Mike. *Leadership Matters: The CEO Survival Manual*. Parker, Colo.: Outskirts Press, 2008.

Mycoskie, Blake. *Start Something That Matters*. New York: Random House, 2011.

Peters, Tom. "The Brand Called You." *Fast Company*, August/September 1997, *www.fastcompany.com/28905/brand-called-you*, accessed February 20, 2015.

Poehler, Amy. *Yes Please*. New York: Harper Collins, 2014.

Price, Steven D. *The Quotable Billionaire*. New York: Skyhorse Publishing, 2009

Ramirez, Anthony. "BUSINESS PEOPLE; Chief at Orion Pictures Is Joining Paramount". February 21, 1992. *The New York Times*.

Rao, Vidya. "Paula Deen: I Would Not Have Fired Me." *TODAY*, June 26, 2013, www.today.com/food/paula-deen-i-would-not-have-fired-me-6C10454147, accessed February 25, 2015.

Rath, Tim. *Strengths Finder 2.0*. New York: Gallup Press, 2007.

Roberts, Robert C. and W. Jay Wood. *Intellectual Virtues: An Essay in Regulative Epistemology*. New York: Oxford University Press, 2007.

Roosevelt, Franklin D. Inaugural Address 1933. Inaugural.Senate. Gov. *http://inaugural.senate.gov/swearing-in/address/address-by-franklin-d-roosevelt-1933*.

Roosevelt, Franklin D. "Dedication by Radio of the Will Rogers Memorial in Claremore, Oklahoma. Hyde Park, New York.," November 4, 1938. Online by Gerhard Peters and John T. Woolley, *The American*

Presidency Project. www.presidency.ucsb.edu/ws/?pid=15567, accessed February 24, 2015.

Roosevelt, Theodore. "International Peace." Nobel Lecture, Oslo, Norway, May 5, 1910.

Rubin, Gretchen.*The Happiness Project*. New York: HarperCollins, 2011.

Salzmann, Mary Elizabeth. *Alcott to Zaharias: Famous Women from A to Z.* Edina, Minn.: ABDO Publishing Company, 2009.

Sandberg, Sheryl. *Nightline*. By Cynthia McFadden. ABC News. March 10, 2014.

Santillano, Vicki. "Don't Be Sorry: How to Overcome Over-Apologizing." *DivineCaroline*, 8 June 2010, *www.divinecaroline.com/22189/99668-don-t-sorry-overcome-over-apologizing*, accessed February 20, 2015.

Sawyer, Rebecca. "The Impact of New Social Media on Intercultural Adaptation." Senior Honors Projects, 2011, Paper 242. *http://digitalcommons.uri.edu/srhonorsprog/242.*

Schlesinger, Leonard, Charles F. Kiefer, and Paul B. Brown. *Just Start, Take Action, Embrace Uncertainty, Create the Future*. Boston: Harvard Business Review Press, 2012.

Schumann, Karina and Michael Ross. "Why Women Apologize More Than Men: Gender Differences in Thresholds for Perceiving Offensive Behavior." *Psychological Science* 21 (2010): 1649-1655.

Seuss, Dr. *Happy Birthday to You!* New York: Random House Children's Books, 1959.

Showalter, Amy. *The Underdog Edge: How Ordinary People Change the Minds of the Powerful and Live to Tell About It*. New York: Morgan James Publishing, 2011.

Singh, M.P. *Quote Unquote: A Handbook of Quotations*. New Delhi: Lotus Press, 2006.

Smith, Christie. "The New Connected Leadership." Panel discussion at the 2014 Fortune Magazine's Most Powerful Women Summit, October 6-8, 2014.

Sobel, Robert. *When Giants Stumble: Classic Business Blunders and How to Avoid Them*, Prentice-Hall, 1999.

Stelzner, Michael. "2013 Social Media Marketing Industry Report." *Socialmediamarketing.com*, Social Media Marketing, 2013. *www.socialmediaexaminer.com/SocialMediaMarketingIndustry Report2013.pdf.*

Stevenson, Richard W. "THE MEDIA BUSINESS; New Line Breaks Off Talks On Buying Orion Pictures". *The New York Times*, March 22, 1992. Retrieved 2010-08-08.

Sullivan, John.*1000 Ways To Recruit Top Talent*, Independent, 2009.

Thoreau, Henry D. *Walden*. New York: Thomas Y. Crowell & Co., 1910.

Tichy, Noel, and Ram Charan. "Speed, Simplicity, Self-Confidence: An Interview with Jack Welch." *Harvard Business Review*, September 1989. *https://hbr.org/1989/09/speed-simplicity-self-confidence-an-interview-with-jack-welch*.

"Tiffany & Co. Company History" *International Directory of Company Histories*, Vol. 14. St. James Press, 1996.

Trumbore, Brian. "Discount Retailers." *Buy and Hold*, 2001. *www.buyandhold.com/bh/en/education/history/2001/discount_retailers.html*, accessed February 25, 2015.

Turner, Sherry. "How to Offer Apologies," Mount Holyoke, accessed February 24, 2015, *www.mtholyoke.edu/ombuds/apologies*.

Twain, Mark. *What is Man? And Other Essays*. New York: Harper & Brothers Publishers, 1917.

Tzioumakis, Yannis. *AMERICAN INDEPENDENT CINEMA*. Edinburgh: Edinburgh University Press. 2006.

Tzu, Lao. BrainyQuote.com, Xplore Inc, 2015. *www.brainyquote.com/quotes/quotes/l/laotzu165407.html*, accessed February 23, 2015.

Warrell, Margie. "Afraid of Being 'Found Out?' How To Overcome Imposter Syndrome." On *Forbes.com*, 3 April 2014. *www.forbes.com/sites/margiewarrell/2014/04/03/impostor-syndrome*

Watkins, David B. *Where's My Dog? The Search for Honest Leadership*. Udligenswil, Switzerland: WM Consulting, 2013.

Weinberg, Amber. "The Complainers. The Doers and the Ones Who Succeed." *Amberweinberg.com*, 30 November 2011, *www.amberweinberg.com/the-complainers-the-doers-and-the-ones-that-succeed*.

Weiner, Rex. "MGM Ends Orion Orbit," July 11, 1997. *Variety Magazine*. *http://variety.com/1997/film/news/mgm-ends-orion-orbit-1116676950/*, accessed February 25, 2015.

Wilde, Oscar. BrainyQuote.com, Xplore Inc, accessed February 23, 2015. *www.brainyquote.com/quotes/quotes/o/oscarwilde106826.html*.

Winokur, Jon. *Return of the Portable Curmudgeon*. New York: Plume, 1995.

Zetlin, Minda. "4 Reasons You Should Love Hearing 'No,'" Inc.com, 23 June 2013, *www.inc.com/*

minda-zetlin/4-reasons-you-should-love-hearing-no.html, accessed February 25, 2015.

Ziglar. Zig. Ziglar.com, accessed February 23, 2015. *www.ziglar.com/quotes/you-can-have-everything-life-you-want*.

Zimmerman, Eileen. "The Problem with Pointing Fingers," *New York Times*, 12 March 2011, *www.nytimes.com/2011/03/13/jobs/13careers.html*, accessed February 20, 2015.

Index

About the Author

TAMARA JACOBS is the founder and president of Tamara Jacobs Communications, Inc., an internationally renowned strategic communications firm. An acknowledged expert in the field of high-impact communications, Ms. Jacobs helps her clients "C" their future and realize their potential through *Coaching* for performance, *Conducting* high impact workshops, *Consulting* on issues management, *Corporate* reputation, product positioning, and media pull-through, *Coordinating* agencies, internal/external stakeholders, and *Creating* memorable and targeted messaging.

Tamara incorporates her unique background as an equity actress, news professional, respected journalist, and successful senior executive with a Fortune 500 company into a transformational relationship with her clients. Her approach is designed to shift the focus from "me to we" leadership, promote "rapport with a purpose™," and ultimately take her business partners from informing to inspiring and aligning.

With more than 3,000 keynotes and workshops to her credit, Tamara's theories on personal branding have been captured in her popular guide to executive presence, *Be the Brand*; her highly rated CD-ROM, Effective Presentation, The Power of Organized Conversation; and her rule book for inclusive meetings, *Enlist to Lead*. Tamara's articles on personal impact have been featured in the *New York Times* and such popular magazines as *Fortune*, *Family Circle*, *Victoria Magazine*, *Woman's Day*, and *Woman's World*. She has also been a repeat guest on *World News Tonight*, MSNBC, *Inside Edition*, *Entertainment Tonight*, *Your World with Neil Cavuto*, Fox News, and is a featured contributor to the *Huffington Post*.

Tamara's successful partnerships have molded countless careers and promoted her high-profile clients into senior leadership positions at marquee companies across industries and diverse sectors from pharmaceutical to financial to retail powerhouses. A representative list includes: Amgen, Bayer, BlackRock, Bristol Myers Squibb, JP Morgan Chase, Coty, Johnson & Johnson, Latham and Watkins, Liz Clairborne, Merck, Novartis, Pfizer, Revlon, and Roche.

A passionate trailblazer, Ms. Jacobs uses the unique insights she gained as a rising corporate star to create and share concepts that are instantly applicable. She does not take a "one way, right way" approach. Every relationship is customized and "hand crafted," built on commitment, connectivity, and commonly held values and goals. Tamara's promise is to partner, not pander. Her relationships are candid and constructive, with trust as the cornerstone and call to action as the outcome. Invariably, the benefits derived from these keynotes, small group, and one-on-one sessions are leveraged and shared with the rest of the organization, elevating performance at all levels.

A summa cum laude graduate of the University of Michigan, Ms. Jacobs also attended Mt. Holyoke College, where she was awarded the prestigious distinction of Sarah Williston Scholar. Her interests and activities are broad and varied, from community activist, to political consultant, to serving as a former judge for the Miss America Pageant, to being selected for The Women's Leadership Board, Kennedy School of Government, Harvard University. Married for 28 years to investment banking executive David Epstein, Tamara is the proud mother of Avery, a Syracuse University Music Theatre graduate (BFA), who is pursuing a professional music theatre career.